# Bound by Love, Not Tradition

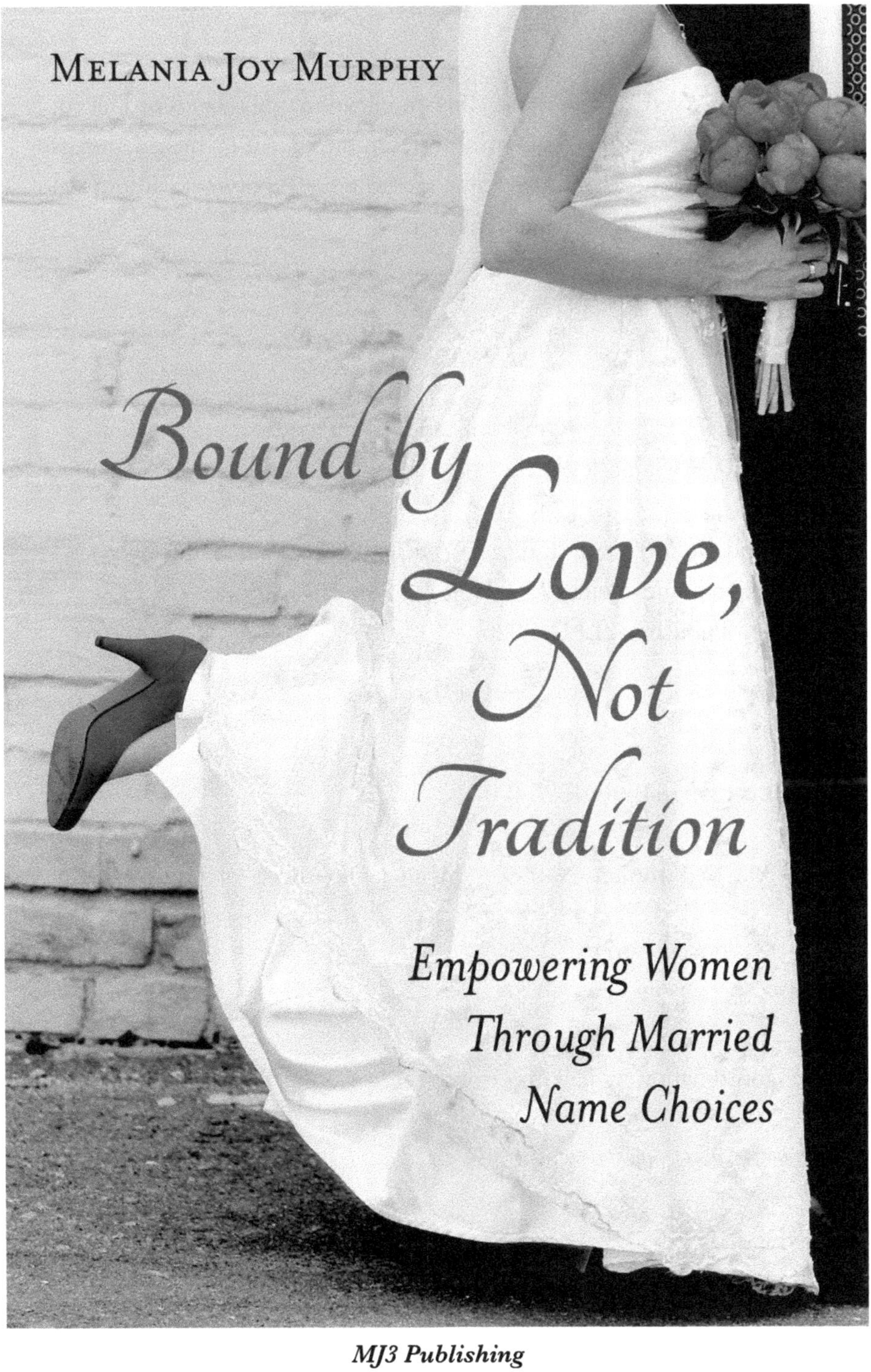


*MJ3 Publishing*
*Bradenton, FL*

Published by
MJ3 Publishing | Bradenton, FL

Publisher's Cataloging-in-Publication Data
Murphy, Melania Joy.

Bound by love, not tradition : empowering women through married name choices / Melania Joy Murphy – Bradenton, FL : MJ3 Publishing, LLC, 2026.

p. ; cm.

ISBN13: 978-0-9601323-0-0

1. Married women--Names. 2. Women--Identity.

HQ1206.M87 2025
155.633--dc23

Project coordination by Jenkins Group, Inc. | www.jenkinsgroupinc.com

*Design by Brooke Camfield*

Printed in the United States of America
30 29 28 27 26 • 5 4 3 2 1

# *Dedication*

For all the women who fought so gallantly and tirelessly for women's rights—from Lucy Stone and Ida B. Wells to Gloria Steinem, Alice Walker, Patsy Mink, Ruth Bader Ginsberg, Malala Yousafzai, and so many more.

For the women who are still fighting today.

And for the women who will continue to fight in the future.

# *Contents*

# Introduction

I love that you picked up this book. It means you're curious about married name choices. Whether you're a first-time bride who hasn't decided what you're doing with your name yet or a repeat bride wondering whether there are other options you haven't considered, I hope you'll find this topic as fascinating as I have researching and writing it.

Or maybe you're a soon-to-be groom who is curious about this topic from a woman's perspective. Welcome. I applaud your curiosity, and don't worry—I think you'll find this book entertaining too.

Choosing your married name is a highly personal decision based on many factors such as your values, phase of life, family customs, and even religion. So many women have told me they've struggled because they want to be true to themselves but they don't want to disappoint their soon-to-be hubby. Or they've built a personal brand and don't want to change it but also want to share a last name with the men they love and their future children. One woman said she got so much pressure from her future in-laws and society that she finally gave in and took his name.

I wrote this book because I feel a woman's worth, identity, and ancestry are as important as those of the man she's about to marry. I want to help you feel empowered—to think clearly about what you want and have the guts and ammunition to ask for it. I want to help you be big and bold and put yourself first while being compassionate, loving, and respectful of all those around you.

But let's be clear, there is no right or wrong answer when it comes to married name choices, only what's best for you and your future spouse.

It wasn't too long ago that you would have been required to take your husband's name. But today in the US, there are no longer any laws requiring women to change their names or men to keep theirs. And the laws stating that a married couple's children must have the father's last name have also been abolished. As Americans, we're lucky because we have the freedom to choose, which isn't the case in many other countries.

But with all our free will, about 80% of women still drop their birth surnames and take on their husband's last name, according to a 2023 Pew Research Study—a statistic that hasn't changed much since the 1970s, when a wave of feminism saw 17% of women keep their birth surname when getting married. What used to be laws are now traditions that are deeply embedded in our society.

This book will dig into that statistic to explain why so many couples still follow that practice; how a 50/50 split between women and men changing their names would affect gender equality in our society; how we achieve that goal in the face of obstacles like traditions, other people's feelings, and expectations for ourselves or by others; and how societal norms get in the way.

To explore those questions, I created a framework called SELF, which stands for Significance, Empowerment, Legacy, and Freedom. Each chapter will dive into one of the components to help you uncover things about yourself you may find surprising.

- Significance: What is the significance of your name in your life and personal story?
- Empowerment: Do you feel empowered to put yourself first and ask for what you want?
- Legacy: What legacy do you wish to create with your name?
- Freedom: Can you enjoy the freedom to choose what feels right for you?

## Attitudes Are Shifting . . . Slowly

Imagine: your husband dies and you're suddenly on your own with three children under the age of five. Amid your grief and despair, you haven't considered what it means to be a widowed mother in a patriarchal society, until you apply for a credit card.

The bank denies your application because your husband's name isn't included. You confess your husband has passed away. The teller indifferently explains that your husband's name must be on the credit card application because you are a married woman.

The conundrum is almost funny. In order to get a credit card in your own name, your dead husband must apply for it with you, which is literally, physically, impossible. This was my mom's situation in 1968. What option did she have in a man's world? She added her late husband's name to the application and forged a dead man's signature. In the US in 1968, a dead man's signature held more power than a living, breathing woman.

We can celebrate how far we've come since the late '60s. Sure, women can get credit cards, but has the power of a man's name versus a woman's name really changed that much?

In the 1980s, a woman keeping her birth surname after marriage was a growing, but still small, practice seen by many as a feminist statement. While more women chose this path than in previous decades, they faced a cultural backlash that challenged the forward motion of the women's movement.

Men who wanted to assert their authority would often demand that their fiancées take their last names, and when Bill Clinton lost his bid for reelection as governor of Arkansas in 1980, one of the issues that critics used against him was his wife's decision to keep her maiden name, which was seen as unconventional and offensive by some Arkansas voters.

Over the past couple of decades, society's attitudes have shifted to respecting a name change as a woman's decision.

I worked with a man, Steve, who told me that when he got married in 2019, he was very supportive of his wife and whatever she wanted to do with her name. He said it was completely up to her if she wanted to keep her name, take his, or hyphenate and he would support her all the way.

I commended Steve for his maturity and respect for his wife's decision but then asked him, "If it was important to your wife that both of you and your future children all have the same last name and she really wanted to keep her own, would you consider changing your name?"

He looked at me completely shocked and said, "No, why would I change my name?"

Steve was right. Why would he change his name? We live in a world where a wife taking a husband's name is so normal. Why wouldn't Steve be proud of being a progressive and supportive husband? His thoughts had evolved over those of men who, decades earlier, would have demanded that a wife assume a husband's surname.

Like Steve, boys and girls receive the same messages growing up—from doodling your name with a boy's last name to having an elementary school teacher explain why her name has changed—when women get married they change their last names. There still aren't enough examples for kids to learn that both men and women have choices. But society's attitudes are slowly changing.

A 2024 survey conducted by the Knot, the Female Quotient, and SmithGeiger Group reported that only 64% of nonmarried women expect to take their husband's last name compared to the 80% reported a year earlier by Pew Research. Can we get to a 50/50 split of women and men changing their names by 2050? How would that shift the power in women and men?

## The Way It Should Be

Now imagine: while planning your wedding, the man you're about to marry initiates a conversation about your married name choices. He says it's important to him for the two of you to have the same last name, especially if you have children. But he understands that your last name holds as much meaning to you as his last name does for him. He explains that he is willing to explore all options, including him taking your name or hyphenating both names, just as long as it's fair and equal and you're both happy with the decision.

But how often is that the reality? I've talked to hundreds of people about how they chose their married names, and practically no one dealt with that idyllic scenario. Most soon-to-be brides say their groom wants her to take his name and she's planning to do it because of a myriad of different reasons, such as to feel united, to be respectful, to have the same family name as her future children, or . . . fill in the blank.

And there's nothing wrong with choosing to take your husband's name EXCEPT when it's assumed you'll take his name because it's tradition or the way it should be. I bet you have friends or family members who didn't even discuss all the options available to them.

Nick Bets, a cybersecurity specialist, who married a nurse in 2021, told me, "My wife and I both assumed we would take my name. I don't think my wife had any pressure or emphasis to decide. In fact, I don't think she felt she was making a decision. I'm sure she felt the same way as I did and assumed she would be taking my name. I also believe she would have wanted my name anyway, but this is an educated guess."

Sam Scriver, a science teacher, who married a doctoral student in 2019, said, "We didn't really talk about it much before we got married, but she did say once that it would be weird having a different last name. Now that we're married, I asked her again, and she said that she wanted to change her last name because our kids would have my last name and she wanted all of us to have the same last name."

## My Story

When I got married at age 21, my ex and I sounded just like these couples. We never had a conversation, and I nonchalantly dropped my birth surname and took on his. After legally changing my name with the Social Security

Administration and updating my driver's license, I needed to update my name on one checking account and one credit card. It wasn't too difficult because I was young.

But when I got married a second time at 40, life was more complicated. Over the 20 years since my first name change, I had earned my bachelor's and master's degrees, had published articles, owned multiple credit cards and investments, held a passport, and, most importantly, raised three wonderful children. All my college classmates, coworkers, PTO parents, and social media "friends" know me by my married name. My name had a lot more significance at this stage in my life. It had been my identity practically my entire adulthood. The second time around, I kept the name I adopted at my first wedding.

Growing up, I lived in a blended household with different family names under the same roof. My dad passed away from complications of juvenile diabetes when I was 3 years old. When my mom married my stepfather, she took his last name, while my siblings and I kept our dad's surname. I saw firsthand as a kid how people in the same house could have different last names and still be a family.

While earning my degree in applied behavioral science, I learned about the dynamics of how people relate to each other and applied that information to this topic. Over my 20 years as a journalist, I've interviewed hundreds of people and have used those skills to have conversations with people and experts about married name choices. I've published articles in national publications and discussed the topic on multiple podcasts. It is my pleasure to share all that information with you now, in this book.

## Author's Note

Where possible, I changed names of individuals to protect their privacy. If I used a person's real name, I was given permission.

# chapter one
# SELF
# Today

"I don't think I'm going to change my name when we get married," I casually mentioned to my fiancé while setting the dinner table. We both had been married before and had already combined our teenage kids into the new house we bought together.

Life was a little crazy coordinating doctor appointments, sports schedules, and other incidentals that came along with managing a household of eight and working full time. The chore of changing my name seemed overwhelming.

While holding the stack of plates, my fiancé stopped, wrinkled his forehead with inquiry, and asked, "But then how will people know you're married to me?"

"Well, probably the same way people will know you're married to me," I said as I brought the knives and forks to the table. "They'll see we wear wedding rings. We'll tell them we're married, and we'll refer to each other as husband and wife."

He sat down on the chair at the end of the table and lowered the stack of plates, still processing the concept. Although we were both in our forties, it was the first time he had considered his wife not taking his name. "Huh, okay. I guess I just thought you would change your name when we got married."

"Yeah, I know," I said, trying to be sensitive, considering this was a completely new idea to him. "I mean, I love the idea of both of us having the same last name, but it's not that easy," I said while placing the silverware around the absent plates and walking around him at one end of the table.

After a few seconds of contemplating, he put his elbow on the table, propped his chin up with his fist, and curiously asked, "But won't that be weird if we have different last names?"

"Possibly, but I want to have the same last name as my children, and I wouldn't want them to feel like I'm leaving them behind and switching to your family," I said, remembering how it felt when my mom took my stepfather's name when I was growing up. I playfully suggested, "If you want, you can change your name to my last name."

He scoffed at that suggestion, stood up, started placing the plates with a resounding clunk, and said, "I'm not going to take your ex-husband's last name."

Oh, I hadn't thought of it like that. Since I had this identity for so long, I didn't associate it with my ex-husband.

"I see your point because I really wouldn't want to have your ex-wife's last name either," I said, taking a couple steps sideways so he could get by with the plates. He stopped and looked up. His head was tilted, his eyebrows were creased, and with a puzzled look he finally chuckled, "What?" He then shrugged his shoulders, slightly shook his head, and went back to placing the plates.

I continued to add options to keep the conversation going. "We could both change our names to one from my family tree," I suggested.

"How about Schulze?" I asked.

"Schulze?!" he spouted. "I'm not German. I'm Irish."

At that point I had a mix of emotions: shock at the mocking of my heritage and comic relief as I imagined Shultz, the German guard from the reruns of the '60s sitcom *Hogan's Heroes* with his round face and egg-shaped army green helmet.

"Haha, you're definitely not a Shultz! And I'm not Irish, even though I've had an Irish name for more than half my life."

At this, we both started laughing at where the conversation had ended up. "Well, if we each keep our last names, at least we'll both have Irish last names."

As we brought the food to the table and the kids started to gather, we stood back and admired the eclectic, blended family we had created. This conversation taught me a lot about the significance of our names. Neither of us wanted to change our surnames, and that's what worked best for us.

## Remove Gender from the Equation

Are you like many soon-to-be brides who want to share a unified name with their husband, whether that name is his, yours, a combination, or a new name? Have you considered all your options?

One couple I'll introduce you to later flipped a coin at the altar to determine which of their surnames to take. Another couple created a new family name years after they were married and had a family-versary by legally changing the wife's, husband's, and kids' family name.

I want to encourage you to come to the married name discussion table on an equal playing field. Once you take gender out of the decision, priorities shift, options open up, and a veil is lifted on possibilities. But you may be asking, What exactly does that mean?

Consider LGBTQIA+ couples and their conversations about married name choices compared to heterosexual couples. They don't have the baggage reminding them that years ago one person and her children were property of the other person and that brides were required to change their last name.

A recent survey by the Knot, the Female Quotient, and SmithGeiger Group unveiled that one person in a LGBTQIA+ couple took the other person's name 53% of time, while 26% of couples chose to keep their individual last names. It mentions that in LGBTQIA+ relationships there's no precedent dictating who should change their last name to whose and that they share the decision-making process, leaning into factors like individuality, mutual equality, aesthetics, and more.

Bridget and Katy live in Tucson, Arizona, and each kept their birth surnames when they married. Once they had a child, they hyphenated both their surnames as his last name. They did the same thing with their daughter, and both women socially use the hyphenated last name.

Bridget and Katy had different reasons for wanting to keep their birth surnames, and all were valid. There was no pressure from one person "encouraging" the other to take their last name. There were no "hurt feelings" from families because one person did not take the other's name. And neither felt shame by not following a societal norm that didn't exist for them.

Both women were respectful of each other's decision, and together they came up with a solution for their family name.

Wouldn't it be great if heterosexual couples approached the married name discussion the same way? Instead, there is so much pressure on women to conform to societal norms. Even if her fiancé is open to a non-traditional choice, families and society burden women—and men, for that matter—to stay in the established gender roles.

By taking gender out of the equation, you're left with two equal humans determining what's best for themselves and their future family.

It's hard to figure out what you want when the noise of everything around you is telling you what to do. By working through the SELF framework, you'll be able to examine yourself and your world in a safe, nonjudgmental, gentle space to clearly see what would work best for you and how to make that your reality.

*chapter two*

# SELF SIGNIFICANCE,

*empowerment,*

*legacy,*

*freedom*

Let's explore the significance of your name in your life and personal story. A name is more than just a label; it's a fundamental part of your identity, reflecting cultural heritage, personal history, and how you are perceived and addressed by others, making it a crucial element of human interaction and self-understanding.

For women, we have been taught that a last name is like a sticky note placed on our foreheads—it's not always permanent. It's temporarily stuck on and can just as easily be taken off.

Jennifer Lopez is a great example. When she married Marc Anthony (born Marco Antonio Muñiz), she legally changed her name to Jennifer Muñiz, then switched it back to Lopez when they divorced.

When she married Ben Affleck (born Benjamin Géza Affleck-Boldt), she officially changed her name to Jennifer Affleck. She later got divorced and signed court papers to revert to Jennifer Lopez once again.

She gets married and slaps another name on her legal documents. She gets divorced and that temporary name is removed. For her, that last name is all about the romance.

In a November 2022 interview with *Vogue*, she said, "People are still going to call me Jennifer Lopez. But my legal name will be Mrs. Affleck because we're joined together. We're husband and wife. I'm proud of that. I don't think that's a problem."

Jennifer Lopez seems to have put significance to each of her names. Jennifer Lopez—JLo—is her brand, stage name, business identity. But her name in relationships changes with her husband's as a romantic gesture.

## The Whole Wedding Package

JLo isn't the only one who likes the romance of a wife taking a husband's last name. Many women began dreaming of their wedding day when they were little girls.

My friend's daughter, Amanda, started her wedding vision board on Pinterest before she was even engaged, just like so many other bride wannabes. She collected images of gorgeous white strapless wedding gowns, woven and braided updos with sprigs of baby's breath tucked in the back, and colorful bouquets with flowers and greens cascading like peacock feathers. She had pictures of shoes, color palettes, bridesmaids' dresses, cakes, invitations, and wedding party thank-you gifts.

Then there were the venues. She wanted to be married in a field with the mountains or maybe a lake behind her. But of course, she would need a tent to protect everyone from Mother Nature. The twinkly light designs and the drapery and greenery choices were magnificent. The options for centerpieces, place settings, and guest books with table cards were overwhelming. She had collected ideas for everything, even a tuxedo for her dog.

She said that she had been dreaming of her wedding day since she was a little girl, and she couldn't believe her dream was finally coming true. She had found the perfect man, he proposed on one knee, and she couldn't wait to take his name.

All these elements have come to form part of the optimum "marriage package" for many couples. "It's all part of the romance," Corinna Hirsch said in a BBC article. She, too, took her husband's last name when they married a year before. "We slept in separate rooms the evening before the wedding. I had something old, blue, borrowed, and new. My dad and husband gave a speech, but I didn't." She believes these traditions helped her and her fiancé develop a deeper bond, even after more than eight years together. "We didn't expect that we would feel any closer after the wedding, but I think having this big wedding and having one last name did the trick."

She's not alone. For many women, taking a husband's last name when they get married wraps the whole romantic wedding package up in a unifying bow.

When a colleague of mine was asked what she would put in a hypothetical time capsule, she said, "Our wedding rings so they know I was wifey material," implying that her identity is associated with her image of what a woman "should" be.

Another woman said she would add "a photo album from my (future) wedding day, filled with photos of the most important people in my life—and one special photo of my wedding dress. This album would freeze one of the most joyful, love-filled days of my life in time. It wouldn't just be about the dress or the venue but the people who stood beside us, the love we felt, and the memories that shaped the start of our forever. The one photo of my wedding dress would remind me of how beautiful I felt that day, inside and out, and how excited I was to become a Bleull."

Movies like *Mamma Mia!*, *Crazy Rich Asians*, and even the iconic series *Friends* school us on wedding "shoulds and shouldn'ts." But it's true: you can change your name to Princess Consuela Banana Hammock or Crap Bag if you choose.

"I think the wedding industry, Hallmark movies, and rom-coms do a very good job of making 'taking someone's name' to be a highly romantic act—like an act of being 'really in' the relationship," said Lauren Napolitano, PsyD, a licensed psychologist. "When I got married (and later divorced) 20+ years ago, my own mother pleaded with me not to change my name, citing that it's a ridiculous tradition and that it's antifeminist. I, at 26, however, wanted to impress my husband by showing him how 'all in' I was in our marriage and happily changed my name. It was a way of 'proving' the permanence of our marriage. But I recall as we were engaged many friends, family members, even the priest who married us all asking 'Are you changing your name?' as if they were asking 'You're not going to be one of those dumb feminists who is going to confuse your future children by having a different name, are you?' And I was so proud to say, 'Of course I'm changing my name!' It was an act of people-pleasing for me (and probably rebelling against my mother too). Ultimately, the marriage was doomed, and then I had to go through the extensive paperwork to return my name to my maiden name, so the joke was on me."

And the joke may be on many other women too. In a HuffPost article, Gillian Gualtera explains what she calls the "wedding industry" complex. After analyzing every Disney movie with a princess theme, reading promotional materials from Disney wedding venues, and interviewing 30 newlywed brides, she said, "[Women have] been fed that cookie-cutter 'dream' event from the moment we first watched a Disney movie where a princess is saved by a big, powerful prince.

"Disney starts young, shaping little girls' dreams of being princesses who then dream of being brides," Gualtera said. "TV shows and magazines pound home the same princess message. I was amazed to learn that there are Disney venues one can go to and pretend to be a princess while being a bride, literally starting married life in a fantasy world."

Girls are not the only victims of the Disney image, according to Sarah M. Coyne, PhD. In a Psychology Today article, she reported on male superhero body types and behaviors, such as aggressive-masculinity stereotypes and the muscular ideal. "Interestingly, stereotypes about girls are usually based on physical appearance, whereas for boys stereotypes are based on behavior," she said. "Women need to *look* a certain way, whereas boys need to *act* a certain way."

These gender roles are internalized early. In fact, *Brides* magazine found that approximately 25% of its readers are not yet engaged. TheKnot.com said approximately 37% of the "brides" who visited their site did not have a fiancé.

Sami Horneff from Manhattan said in a *New York Times* article that although she's not engaged yet, she plans to have 150–200 guests at her wedding at the Breakers in Palm Beach, Florida, during the second weekend of some future June. She will drift down the aisle to Pachelbel's "Canon in D," dazzling in a form-fitting, strapless satin dress, a floor-length veil traipsing behind her. Later, guests will nibble on passed hors d'oeuvres and cocktails, followed by an elaborate sit-down dinner.

"I love the idea of weddings and ceremonies and feeling like a princess," Sami said. "I love the idea of being in love. I love fireworks. It's the most amazing thing to commit yourself to someone and share it with the world."

Emily Fairchild, an associate director of undergraduate studies in the Department of Sociology at Harvard University, suggests that for some people, living happily ever after has to do with living in a way that is consistent with social expectations. Along those lines, women who have conflicted feelings about changing their names may believe that by doing so, it will increase their happiness.

"Women are expected to desire and be especially invested in weddings," she said. "The associations among weddings, romance, and femininity are powerful cultural forces that can be difficult to resist. By having a wedding, you prove your worthiness, your womanness, in a way that a man doesn't need to. A man can be a man by having a job, in ways that aren't tied to his family."

Sami also says she holds Walt Disney responsible for her fantasies. "I grew up on Disney, and Disney made me think of princesses," she said. "And what do princesses do? They get married and live happily ever after."

In a culture in which wedding gowns inspired by Disney characters like Belle or Ariel really exist and the designer Christian Louboutin unveiled an actual glass slipper, it's easy to blame *the most magical place on earth* and get swept up in the fairy tales.

In fact, over 4,000 couples per year (that's 11 ceremonies per day) create their dream-come-true wedding on Disney properties, including at Disneyland in California, Walt Disney World in Florida, and Disney's Aulani resort in Hawaii, as well as on multiple Disney cruise lines. According to their website, DisneyWeddings.com, "We've brought love stories to life in truly magical ways for over 30 years—and we can't wait to help you with yours!"

If marrying your Prince Charming and becoming Princess Charming is on your bucket list, all the more power to you. If that's your dream, what better day to make it a reality than on your wedding day?

## Married Names of Disney Princesses

Spoiler alert: If you don't want the Charming bubble to burst, skip the next paragraph. All others, read on for fun Disney princess facts.

Although princesses get married and live happily ever after, do they take Prince Charming's last name?

### *Princesses Who Changed Their Names*

**Pocahontas:** While her actual birth name was Mico (or potentially another undisclosed name), she was given the nickname Pocahontas and then renamed Rebecca after converting to Christianity and marrying John Rolfe.

**Jasmine:** In the movie *Aladdin and the King of Thieves*, Jasmine is married to an unnamed prince, and it is implied that she takes on a new title related to the kingdom, even though her name is not explicitly changed.

### *Princesses Who Did Not Change Their Names*

**Snow White:** She is known by her name, Snow White, after her marriage to the Prince.

**Aurora/Briar Rose:** Her official name is Aurora, and she is known by that name after her marriage to the Prince.

**Cinderella:** She is known by her name, Cinderella, after marrying the Prince, and she is referred to as Princess Cinderella.

**Rapunzel:** She is Princess of Corona and is known as Rapunzel after her marriage to Eugene.

**Tiana:** She is known as Princess Tiana after her marriage to Naveen, and it is implied she becomes Princess of Maldonia.

**Merida:** She is Princess Merida of Clan DunBroch.

**Moana:** While she was given a surname in development, it was never used in the film.

**Belle:** She is known as Belle after her marriage to the Beast, and it is implied she becomes Princess of Castle.

**Mulan:** She does not have a royal connection but is still considered a princess.

One last note from Gualtera's HuffPost piece: "I worry about the not-very-hidden meaning in the princess complex sold by the 'wedding industry.' If the grown-up woman is a princess, what message is she giving her groom about the form and content of their marriage? That she needs to be saved, to be pampered, to be the star of the show? If that's the kind of marriage a woman wants, the wedding industry's princess fantasy is a perfect ceremony. But if a woman wants a marriage with a partner who respects her as an equal, the 'wedding industry' dream walks her down the wrong aisle. And those Disney movies we show little girls just may start them on their road to a dream wedding that leaves them in debt, and a princess rather than a partner."

## Many Reasons to Change Your Name

People change their names for many reasons other than romance and marriage, but the significance behind a name change can be as varied as the individuals who make them, reflecting personal, cultural, and societal nuances.

For celebrities like Ben Affleck and Marc Anthony, as well as Jonah Hill (born Jonah Hill Feldstein) and Whoopi Goldberg (born Caryn Elaine Johnson), legally changing their birth name was a career strategy.

When Kelly Clarkson legally changed her name to Kelly Brianne after divorcing Brandon Blackstock, the significance of her name change was personal. Brianne is her middle name, and while Kelly said that she's still Kelly Clarkson professionally, her new name "more fully reflects who I am."

When Miley Cyrus legally changed her name, the significance, it seems, was a better fit. She was born Destiny Hope Cyrus. On an episode of Netflix's *My Next Guest Needs No Introduction with David Letterman*, she explained that when she was a kid, she was happy all the time, so her family used to call her "Smiley," which turned into "Miley." Then, in 2008, she petitioned to change her name to Miley Ray Cyrus. "My parents thought it was my destiny to bring hope to the world," she told David Letterman. "It is lovely. It is a lot. But I do think that from the beginning it set an intention, which we don't always have."

Putting stardom aside, ordinary people change their names every day for many reasons other than marriage. No one keeps an annual tally of these transformations, said Bruce Lansky, author of several books about names, including *100,000+ Baby Names*, though he estimates it's about 50,000 a year outside of marriage, considering that approximately two million people get married in the US each year and roughly half are choosing to change, add, or rearrange one of their names.

The other 49,999 noncelebrity people who choose to change their legal names each year do it for an array of motivations but mainly because they want the significance of their name to match their identity. It's perfectly legal unless it is for fraudulent or deceptive purposes.

A name change can happen simply because a person doesn't like the name he or she was given at birth. Perhaps they would prefer something more unique than Sue or Bob or something less unique than Elon Musk's son's name X Æ A-Xii.

In this same vein, people with monikers that could be embarrassing, especially if mispronounced or misspelled, may also seek a fresh start.

One woman told me, "I was born with the last name of Niswonger (pronounced Nice-wonger), so there were lots of jokes. Then I married a man with the last name of Meth (like the drug, but I had never heard of the drug back then). After I divorced, I legally changed my name to my middle name of Lynn. After I married my late husband, I kept my legal name of Lynn. After several years of marriage, I finally changed my last name to Jungels. I love my last name! Although I laugh and think it sounds like an exotic dancer."

Others with names that are identifiably ethnic sometimes request name changes for various reasons, including ease of pronunciation and spelling. On the other hand, some individuals would like to reclaim their ethnic heritage by returning to a surname that may have been lost over the years or by the adoption of a new one.

The renowned artist Frida Kahlo, born Magdalena Carmen Frieda Kahlo y Calderón, often used her middle name, Frida, as a way to emphasize her German Mexican heritage. She was born to a German father and a Mexican mother. Initially, she used the name Frieda, which is a German name meaning "peace." At age 25, she dropped the *e* and began using the name Frida to assert her Mexican identity more strongly, particularly in the context of rising Nazi Germany.

A friend shared the story of her identity with her name:

> Coler is my maiden name, but it comes from the common Jewish name Cohen. The story my family tells is that it was either intentionally changed when arriving in America in order to avoid discrimination or it was simply an Ellis Island clerical error that has impacted all generations of Colers since.
>
> Giving up Coler means that people will no longer ask me about my unusual name, which means my identity as half Jewish is no longer visible. People have asked about my unusual last name all my life. I love that people don't know how to pronounce it, and I love sharing my story when people ask.
>
> My identity as half Jewish is so important to me that I wrote my MA thesis on Judaism. To go deeper on why I feel so connected to my last name and my Jewish identity is very emotional. My parents divorced when I was 4 years old. My mom got custody, and I only saw my dad and

> his side of the family every other weekend. My mom is a challenging personality, and her mother was physically abusive. My dad is my hero. This is partly why I'm so in love with my last name. It was one thing I could keep with me always from my dad.

These examples highlight how names can play a significant role in reflecting and connecting an individual to their cultural identity, serving as a link that bridges the gap between personal history and/or ethnic background.

As women, we often downplay our own importance because we want to be more accommodating or "it's just easier" to put our feelings aside for the greater good of the group/family/marriage/other commitments.

When I talked to Nadia, I felt she did just that when she told me the story of how she and her husband decided on a married name.

"Once we started dating, then living together, we got engaged, so it was like, 'I'm committed to this man; I want to be with him,' so I just decided it would make sense to change my name so we could be a unified couple," Nadia said nonchalantly.

"My last name doesn't have any significant cultural value to me," Nadia said. "When my ancestors came over from Yugoslavia in the early 1900s, their last name was Craioveanue, but they changed it to Cravene to be more Americanized. So the name Cravene is just one of those names made up over time. It really doesn't stand out to me as something I need to keep for historical value."

Her tone changed to a more serious one when she began speaking about her husband's name. "Mitchell's last name means a lot to him," she said. "It's an old German last name that is also from Florence. His family is from Florence. It has a lot more historical meaning and value than my last name. It's kind of nice to adopt something that has so much significance to him."

On TikTok, a young man named Jake wanted to show how much he respected and appreciated his stepfather. On his stepdad's fifty-fifth birthday, Jake surprised him with court papers showing he had legally added his stepfather's surname, Sample, to his own.

For many transgender individuals, changing their name is a transformative part of their journey, aligning their outward identity with their inner sense of gender. Names can be changed to the masculine or feminine form of the current name, or they can be entirely new.

Kareem Abdul-Jabbar (born Ferdinand Lewis Alcindor Jr.), the basketball legend, and Muhammad Ali (born Cassius Clay), the boxing champion, changed their names after converting to Islam. Whether it's due to a religious conversion or to honor a deity, name changes for religious reasons are common.

## Following Tradition

My dad passed away when I was 3. He was 36 and died from kidney failure as a result of juvenile diabetes. At the time, my older brother was 4, my younger sister was 1, and my mom was pregnant with my younger brother. My dad was sick for quite a while as his kidneys deteriorated. My siblings and I spent more and more time at my grandma's house, which was only a few miles away. After he passed, my mom moved us in permanently with my grandma.

Four years later, my mom married my stepdad, and my siblings and I moved into his house in the next town over, about 10 miles away from my grandma. I was 7 when my mom remarried, so I remember a little bit of that transition. It was chaotic with the changing routines, the new rules in the new house, and a big, loud male energy when I was accustomed to gentle, softer female authorities.

When we switched homes, we also switched schools—from public to Catholic. During one of the first days at the new school, a teacher addressed my mom as Mrs. Vogel, but my last name was Swiger.

When we got home that day, I took my regular position at the kitchen table—the seat on the left-hand side nearest the phone on the wall, with my back to the galley kitchen. While I dunked my chocolate chip cookie into the glass of milk, I randomly asked my mom about her name.

"Mom, why did they call you Mrs. Vogel at school? Why don't we have the same last name anymore?"

I think she was making baked chicken. I could hear the thunk from tapping the excess milk and egg mixture off a chicken piece before she rolled it in the dish of breadcrumbs and then the crinkle of tinfoil as she placed it on the foil-lined baking pan.

"That's what happens when you get married," she said from behind me. "You change your last name to your husband's, so now I'm Mrs. Herbert Vogel."

Odd, I thought. She was still my mom. My brothers, sister, and I were still her kids, but our name was Swiger. That seemed silly to me. I made a mental note not to change my name simply because I got married.

My mom, however, didn't consider keeping my dad's last name in 1972 because, she said, "That's not what you did back then."

I think part of her felt bad about the division in our new blended family—my siblings and I had one name, while my stepdad, his son, and my mom had a different name—but she was doing what was expected of her and following tradition. Besides, she didn't want to upset her new husband or appear as if she wasn't fully committed to this new relationship by keeping the name of her deceased husband.

Like so many women of that generation who were accustomed to prioritizing other people's feelings, my mom had many obstacles to her own personal goals. Most women are born with that innate trait, and then society continues to reinforce its importance. My mom was no exception. She wanted to please everybody—her husband, her kids, her mother, the schoolteachers, the church, her neighbors, and society in general—which meant she followed tradition, societal norms, and the expectations ingrained in her to be a dutiful wife and mother.

Personally, when I first got married at age 21, I nonchalantly gave up my last name and took on my then-husband's name without even having a discussion. I was so wrapped up in "getting married" and planning our wedding that I had forgotten to honor my younger self's promise not to change my name when I got married.

I think I put more thought into whether I was going to breastfeed my first child or have my first son circumcised (which I didn't even know were decisions I needed to make). The topic of my name was literally never mentioned in my wedding plans; it was assumed.

At the time of my marriage, I was a young college student. Besides not being mentioned as a choice I needed to make, it was no big deal to change my legal documents because I didn't have that many. Unlike women who have told me they want to keep their birth surname to honor a parent, I felt different. For me, there wasn't that much significance to that name, as I didn't know him, his family, or his ancestry.

What I didn't realize at the "I'm not too young to get married" age of 21 was that giving up my German surname for an Irish name meant my future kids and their peers would only think of them as Irish.

I talked about our German ancestors, fed my kids bratwurst and sauerkraut, dressed them in lederhosen and dirndls, and even danced the polka with them in the living room, but nevertheless, they identified with their father's Irish lineage over mine.

When my three kids, all in their twenties, got matching shamrocks tattooed on their bodies to bond over their Irish heritage, I felt jealous. So despite my contempt for having something etched into my skin, I made a bet with them. If they could find a German symbol we could all agree on—no pretzels or beer steins—I would get the tattoo with them. We decided to have the German national flower, a cornflower, tattooed as their Mother's Day gift to me. It wasn't what I would call a pleasant experience, but I love having this connection with my kids and sharing this symbol to honor our German ancestors.

Everyone needs to find what works best for their personal situation. A woman I met while having my hair and makeup done for a photo shoot told me her fiancé was planning to take her name. Like me, she had children from a previous marriage and wanted to continue sharing a last name with them. He didn't have kids and wanted to have the same last name as his bride and new family. As a show of love, honor, and affection, he asked whether he could take her name so they could be one united family.

## Men Change Their Names Too

In the 2023 Pew Research study I mentioned earlier, 5% of men either took their wife's name or hyphenated their name with hers. This statistic is beginning to creep up.

Marco Perego, the Italian artist who, in 2013, married Zoe Saldaña (2025 Oscar winner), told her he was proud of her and would be honored to add her name. She became Zoe Saldaña-Perego, and he became Marco Perego-Saldaña.

"I tried to talk him out of it," she said during a 2015 interview with *InStyle*. "I told him, 'If you use my name, you're going to be emasculated by your community of artists, by your Latin community of men, by the world.'"

Her comment stirred up a lot of controversy that she later clarified in a lengthy Facebook post urging people to let go "of some of the limitations we have inherited from the past and forge a new path moving forward." Here is the entire post:

> Fathers, sons, brothers, men everywhere: Your legacy will not perish if you take your partner's surname, or she keeps hers. I've been made aware that a comment I made regarding my marriage has garnered some attention. I felt proud that my husband decided to take my last name as

his own . . . and I his. I shared my hesitation with him when he told me about his decision, not only did he say, "Ah, Zoe, I don't give a shhheeeetttt!!" (with a very strong Italian accent!!), he also asked me, "Why not? What are you so afraid of?" And it made me wonder . . . What am I so afraid of?

Why is it so surprising, shocking, eventful—that a man would take his wife's surname? Women have never been asked if it's OK for them to give up their names—why doesn't that make the news?

Men, you will not cease to exist by taking your partner's surname. On the contrary—you'll be remembered as a man who stood by change. I know our sons will respect and admire their father more because their father led by example.

Gentlemen, I implore you to think outside the box—remove the box altogether. Let's redefine masculinity. A real "man" leads alongside his partner. A real man accepts his mortality. A real man acknowledges that nothing can be done alone.

I hope that the "buzz" behind this topic isn't just for gossip—but an inspiration for us all to look within and see what is truly important.

Let's start by letting go of some of the limitations we have inherited from the past and forge a new path moving forward.

## Significance of Your Name

Think about what your name means to you. Its significance.

There is no right or wrong answer here, only personal observations. I've talked to women who feel very strongly about the name they were given at birth and want to keep it or incorporate it into their married name; others are happy to give it up.

Kelly Sullivan Walden, a dream expert and minister, shared with me how she chose her married name.

"Two weeks before my wedding, 23 years ago, I panicked," she explained. "What on earth was my name going to be? Sullivan was my identity—my heritage. It carried shamrocks, corned beef hash, Guinness, and 'Danny Boy' sung loud (and slightly off-key). It was my grandpa's gravelly Irish wisdom: 'The road to hell is paved with good intentions.' To toss all that just because I was getting married? No way. I wasn't marrying Dana to erase myself. I was marrying him to expand—to become more of who I already was. Cutting off Sullivan felt like cutting off a piece of my soul. But hyphenating? A bit much. So I made Sullivan my middle name and added Walden as my last. Boom. A yes/and, not an either/or. It just felt right."

One woman, Carlene, told me, "I took my husband's surname at the age of 18. I would make the same choice again today. Mogavero is from near Palermo in Sicily and means 'fearsome warrior.' It was an Arabic-influenced word pertaining to mercenaries. I think it's badass. I have researched my husband's ancestors in Sicily to the early 1800s. My maiden name is Rodde, and I have very positive feelings about that name as well and have researched that line of my father's into the 1600s in East Prussia. I'm still not sure what it means, but I like to think it has to do with the oars of Viking ships."

Donna kept her maiden name in both marriages. "I've always loved my last name—Martino. It's distinctive, and it connects me to my Italian roots. When other Italians hear my name, they call me paisano (friend or fellow Italian). There's a comforting sense of belonging to something bigger than myself."

She went on to say, "Growing up in Chicago, Italian culture was everywhere. But when I moved to Colorado, I quickly realized that wasn't true for everyone. I'll never forget a young salesclerk in Boulder who looked at my credit card, paused, and asked, 'Is that eye-talian?' I cringed at the mispronunciation but said yes. Then she said, 'That's so cool.' I laughed—and in that moment, I appreciated my name even more."

Another woman took that scenario a step further. Gloria also moved her birth name to her middle name and added her husband's last name, but she felt it was only fair that he put effort into a unified name, too, and he agreed. He legally changed his middle name to her birth name so they both had the same middle and last names.

## Exercise

Here are some prompts you can use to work through your feelings. At this point, don't let obstacles—like social norms, tradition, expectations, or opinions of other people—influence your thoughts. We'll discuss overcoming them later. Right now, just focus on you and your inner dialogue.

- How does your name distinguish you from others? Is it a key part of your personal identity?

______________________________

______________________________

- Does your name carry the history and traditions of your family and culture?

______________________________

______________________________

- Does your name help foster connections and a sense of belonging in certain communities?

---

---

- Is your name often mispronounced? Is it common or unusual? Is it embarrassing? Does any of this bother you?

---

---

- Does your name carry power or responsibility, and do you like that?

---

---

- Some research suggests that names can even influence life decisions, such as career choices, relationships, and charitable giving. How does this resonate with you?

---

---

# *chapter three*

# SELF

*significance,*

# EMPOWERMENT,

*legacy,*

*freedom*

Be empowered to put yourself first and ask for what you want. Let's face it: culture and society tell women to stay small—don't upset the apple cart. Let's be bold and figure out what married name choices align with our values despite what we've been told.

A woman named Jasmin told me that when she and her husband started talking about last names before they married, he expressed the importance of them sharing the same family name, especially when they had children. The option of him taking her name simply wasn't an alternative in their minds.

"I would say he encouraged me to take his name, but he was understanding of my reservations and didn't push me too much," Jasmin said. "I had hesitations about taking his last name, as I am the only girl in my family and would be the only family member with a different last name. I had built my life and career with my maiden name. However, after considering the importance it held for my husband and our future family, I decided to willingly take his name."

Did Jasmin have a choice? Did she feel empowered to ask for what she wanted? She could have kept her birth surname but then would have been the only one with that name when they had children, as he already implied their future children would have his last name. It's as if a woman is hearing, *You can live in any house you want. I'll be completely supportive, but the kids and I are going to live in this house. But it's up to you. No pressure.*

Jasmin wrestled with the idea of taking his name or, in other words, conforming to societal norms.

"Will changing my last name change who I am?" Jasmin asked herself. "No, it will not change who I am at my core. It won't change my place in my family. It will be so difficult to change my name, with work, Social Security, passport, etc., but this is a one-time change that will require some work, but it's worth it to have the same last name as my husband and future children."

It seems to me that her husband held the power in this situation. Tradition and customs were in his favor. He was going to keep his name and give their children his name. What would you do in Jasmin's situation? "Willingly" take his name so you, your husband, and future children all have the same name or shake things up and present a new option?

Let's try an experiment. Ask yourself this question and then notice your initial reaction.

Picture yourself with your husband. You're celebrating your two-year anniversary, and you're six months pregnant. The two of you are blissfully in love and looking forward to starting your family. You each decided to keep your last names when you got married.

You say to your husband, "When our baby is born, I'd like to give our child my last name."

What's your husband's reaction?

Does he laugh and say, "Haha, very funny"? Is he surprised? Does he dismiss your suggestion? Coming from my generation, I assume he wouldn't say, "OK, that's fair since you have just as much right as I do to name our child."

When you said those words, what did you feel in your body? A knot in your stomach, a defensive stance, or maybe a flutter of excitement?

When I imagined that scenario for the first time, I felt an instant pang of fear. After searching deeper, the reaction came with a message. The thought that I could be so bold, pompous, confident, and secure to challenge that social norm made my muscles cringe as if someone jumped around a corner and yelled, "Boo!"

An image of a man popped into my mind. It wasn't my husband, because he's never shown aggression toward me. But this person was screaming at me. He had so much rage, and I could feel his intimidation. The message he implied was that I was taking something he felt was his birthright.

I have a feeling I'm not the only one with that reaction. Even reminding myself that children, just like wives, are no longer a man's property, didn't ease my fear. So where did that unconscious feeling, that message, come from if I've never experienced aggression or violence personally before?

We see it in movies, TV shows, on social media and the nightly news all the time—the implied or actual violence by men toward women. Even if the woman doesn't get hurt physically, his intimidation through power, strength, and aggression usually does the job. Movies with these themes are often rated PG-13 for all the young teens—male and female—to see. We're teaching our children how society expects them to act. If girls/women step out of place, boys/men can/will impose consequences.

According to the Motion Picture Association, PG-13-rated movies can depict implied violence toward women, although sexual violence should not be depicted unless implied or referenced. We've grown up in a society that stresses the fact that men are usually physically bigger, stronger, and more aggressive than women. It doesn't make them better, just more physically powerful. But history, media, and violent crimes on the news present that fear in very subtle and not-so-subtle ways.

It's hard to feel equal when the message we receive growing up is that men have, and will, continue to use violence to keep women in their place.

## Gender Inequality in Married Names

Chris McDermott, a certified life planner and registered nurse said:

> When societal norms dictate that a man's name, family history, and identity take precedence, it perpetuates a subtle yet powerful message of gender hierarchy. This dynamic can lead to self-worth issues, triggering feelings of inadequacy or diminished value in women who adopt their spouse's name. Such symbolic subordination can fuel anxiety, as women may grapple with a sense of erasure or loss of individual identity.
>
> Furthermore, this practice can foster disempowerment, reinforcing traditional gender roles that limit autonomy. Mental health outcomes are intricately tied to societal perceptions, and challenging these norms by promoting equal naming practices in marriage is vital for fostering positive mental health and bolstering women's sense of self and agency.

There are so many hidden messages built into our culture to suppress women's power that we hardly even recognize them.

A man named Leo told me that when he was first engaged, he told his fiancée that it would be a deal-breaker if she didn't take his last name. He admits he's now divorced and has matured, so he no longer feels that way, but at the time, he was serious.

When I asked him why it was so important for his fiancée to take his name, he said he never stopped to think about that. After a few moments, he said, "My dad would think less of me as a man if my wife didn't take my last name. Huh, I never realized that before."

The message of how a man should act was so ingrained in him that he had to really sit with his feelings before realizing what those unconscious thoughts were.

This is an example of unconscious bias. We all have it. According to Harvard University, unconscious bias is a set of snap judgments we make about people and situations based upon years of subconscious socialization.

Dr. Mahzarin Banaji, a psychologist at Harvard University, points out that the human brain is hardwired to make quick decisions that draw on a variety of assumptions and experiences without us even knowing it is doing so, meaning that our unconscious predispositions can influence our decision-making.

Unconscious bias, also known as implicit bias, is not deliberately or consciously created but rather a product "of our brain's definition of normal, acceptable, or positive, and . . . shaped by many factors—from past experiences to our cultural environment to the influence of our social community and media around us," Banaji said.

A woman named Laura told me that as a society, we tend to assume that a married woman has taken her husband's last name.

"I've always loved my maiden name, but never thought I wanted to keep it because, in my opinion, it makes life way more complicated," Laura said. "I'm sure it has to do with societal norms and traditions."

Laura went on to say: "If I chose not to [take his name], I'd be in the position of always correcting people—which feels awkward to me. As a hypothetical, I think of meeting my husband's acquaintances, who would assume I had the same last name, and then I'd have to correct them that that's not my name. Same with after I have children—my children would have my husband's last name, but mine would be different. And again, I'd have to correct everyone. It puts the burden on me, and it just doesn't seem like it would be worth the effort."

## Data Backing Up the Stories

A study published in June 2024 in *Sexuality and Culture* showed that despite an increase in couples making varied name choices following marriage, cultural attitudes toward nontraditional surname choices remain rooted in sexism. According to the author, women who retain their birth surnames often are viewed negatively as individuals and as partners within their marriages.

Participants read scenarios about a man and woman marrying and choosing different options for married names—traditional versus nontraditional. They were asked to evaluate the man and woman's commitment to the marriage, who had more power in the marriage, the quality of their relationship, and the likelihood of divorce. They also filled out an Ambivalent Sexism Inventory (ASI) to assess participants' level of sexism and demographic information.

The results indicated the perception that women who keep their surnames are considered less committed to their marriages and hold more power in their marriages and that the quality of the marriage was lower. There was no association between women's surname change decisions and estimated likelihood of divorce.

By contrast, men who change their name at marriage were perceived as more committed and holding less power in their marriage. Participants did not perceive a man's name change as an indication of quality or likelihood of divorce.

Results indicated that participants with higher levels of sexism perceived nontraditional surname choices—and the individuals who make those choices—more negatively. These findings underscore the persistent role of sexism in cultural attitudes toward marital surname choices in an emerging adult population.

Although the study was conducted with a small sample, the results supported existing work conducted within the last 20 years suggesting that cultural attitudes are influenced by sexism and that individuals feel the pressure to conform to "patriarchal norms" when choosing whether to retain their birth surnames. Across genders, keeping one's surname in marriage was associated with holding more power in the marital relationship.

In 2017, Emily Fitzgibbons Shafer, a sociology professor at Portland State University, published a study that showed that more than 70% of US adults believed that a woman should change her name after she gets married. The study surveyed a representative national sample of 1,200 adults. She presented the participants with a fictional scenario, in which they were asked to evaluate a hypothetical woman's commitment to being a wife and rate how "justified" her husband would be in divorcing her if she worked late hours at her job. Shafer was particularly interested in how people's values, or unconscious bias, affect their beliefs.

"The most common reason (approximately 50 percent of the cases), given by individuals who advocated women's name change, was the belief that women should prioritize their marriage and their family ahead of themselves," she notes in the study.

She went on to say that while research has shown that women are routinely criticized for acting in their own self-interest (i.e., like men) in the workplace, these new—yet not-so-new—findings confirm that we face backlash for similar reasons in our homes.

"My work shows that women can face backlash at home as well if they're not acting 'properly' as wives," Shafer said.

These beliefs are learned early in life and perpetuated continually through media, politics, and religion.

The Global Early Adolescent Study—a partnership between the Johns Hopkins Bloomberg School of Public Health, the World Health Organization, and the United Nations Population Fund—assessed gender and sexuality in adolescents aged 10 to 14 and found these biases are learned throughout life, but starting in childhood.

"This is an age group that is acutely tuned in to the world around them, and it's the age group when norms of behavior and attitude are becoming ingrained and solidified," says Johns Hopkins pediatrician Robert Blum, the lead author of this study.

The study shared the example of a grandmother giving advice to her 11-year-old granddaughter. "Girls should be economically independent," the woman said. But, she added, marrying a rich man is also an important goal, and once betrothed, a girl must work hard because a man "will divorce you if you don't do housework."

This head-spinning contradiction, the study reports—be financially independent but also marry a rich man and be a good housewife—marks the kind of confusing messages many young girls absorb. They must be educated and pursue a career but also hew to the stringent gender norms ingrained by centuries of social conditioning.

I wanted to do my own mini study to find out what this age group—10 to 14—thought about the tradition of wives taking their husbands' names when they marry. So I asked a class of sixth graders, who are usually around age 11, why they think most women change their names. I love kid answers. They are so blatant and unrefined. They just say it like they see it. I didn't ask the teacher for the names or genders of the respondents, but it's clear that gender norms are already being developed. Can you pick out which answers are from boys and which are from girls?

- Because I don't think they had rights. That means they can't do anything. But I don't know if I'm correct.
- They like the man's last name more or maybe it's just a girl thing, idk.
- Because the man is the one to propose so the woman takes the last name.
- Because women used to not be treated equally and it carried on to now, but I don't really know.
- Cause they don't like their last name. And I think it's a proper thing.
- Because everybody else does and they give in to peer pressure.
- I think that they change their last name because the man is the leader and they follow the leader.
- Because women used to not have rights and they had to listen to their husband so we just stuck with it.
- Because it's a tradition and Maloney sounds cooler than my future wife's name.
- Maybe because they want to have the same last name as their children. They might feel closer to their family while having the same last name.
- Because they want to have a relationship with their husband.
- I think they do because then you know two adults are most likely married if they have the same last name.
- Most women change their last name when married, most likely to feel honored and confirm their relationship; commitment.
- Some woman feel the need to.
- I think most women change their last name when they get married because that can show that they are married. What I mean is that if they are signing a document with their spouse it will become clear that they are married without confusion.

- I think that women change their name because they used to have no rights. They also might have felt like they might be forced.
- Back then the women were considered unimportant and people wanted to have their kids have the husband's last name.
- Because it is just a proper thing to do when you get married.
- To show their love to their husband?
- To show that they are married to someone?????????
- To continue on the man's last name.
- So people know that they are married and feel very a part of the family.
- Because it states that your [sic] married.
- For people to know which man the woman is married to.
- Because it shows honor and loyalty to the man she gets married to, and it's just respect.
- Because she gets to pick out the house and make all the chores.
- They change their last name because they want people to know they are married to that person. It also makes them feel like they are really family and makes them feel more attached.
- I think they change their name because they want to be the same as who they marry. So people aren't confused and so people know they are married to someone.
- I think they change the last name because most people do it or whether they really like whoever they are marrying.
- I think that most women change their last name when getting married to be like a part of the groom's family.
- Most women might change their last name when they become married to signify they are part of their husband's family. They also could change it because they want to feel more connected to their lover.
- I think they change their name so it shows and people know that they are part of that family and they have the same last name as

their husband. It represents them making/starting their family and the next generation.

- They want to be similar to their husband.
- I guess it's like a promise to your partner. And like that you will stay with them forever.
- To pass on a generation.
- I really don't know.

## A More Equitable Approach

Imagine if choosing a married name were approached equally by the couple getting married. Just as they both decide on a wedding date, both decide on the venue, and both agree on a honeymoon destination, they discuss and agree on a married name together.

The shift is slight, but the equality is huge. I've talked to many men about how they and their wives chose their married names. I can tell from their responses that they are being respectful and supportive of the women they love, but their answers are a product of our society.

- I told her she didn't have to take my name.
- I was willing to support whatever decision she made—keep her name or take mine.
- It is her choice and I'm comfortable with and respect her decision.

When I asked the same men whether they would consider changing their names, it was clear they were all raised with the same cultural norms. Their answer was no—they would not change their names.

- Men don't change their names.
- My name is rare and unique and I like it.
- My name is who I am. I don't want to change it.

- Society doesn't expect me to change my name, so, to tell you the truth, I didn't even consider it.
- The emphasis is on women to change because "that's the way it's always been done," regardless of how antiquated that is, and most people dislike being considered "too different."

## Traditions and Expectations

The expectations to follow social norms and traditions can be an obstacle that keeps us from reaching our personal goals; sometimes that can cause awkward situations.

A woman named Jane told me she was struggling with her married name decision. She was very close to her family and wanted to honor that connection by incorporating her birth name, but at the same time she liked the idea of her future children having the same last name as their mother and father.

To complicate the situation, she lived in a part of the country where monograms are still very popular—monogrammed sweaters, monogrammed napkins, monogrammed stationery.

The Southern Rose, a shop in Missouri that loves to personalize everything, had this to say about the trend:

"A popular monogram tradition for married women is to bring with them a series of household items that show off her new name. In the past, these items were part of her dowry and consisted of towels, linens, and more. Today, guests of the wedding often bring the bride and groom a gift that is monogrammed with their nuptial initials. It's a sweet symbol of two people intertwining their lives and a constant reminder of the love they share."

Jane's soon-to-be mother-in-law wanted to be the first to give her an engagement gift with the initials she expected her son's wife to have once they married. Of course, the problem was that Jane hadn't decided what those initials were going to be yet.

"Oh my gosh, it was so uncomfortable," Jane said about the monogrammed cloth napkins. "I love Bill's mom, and it was so nice of her to give me this gift, but I wish people wouldn't assume women are going to automatically change their names."

The pressure to please her fiancé as well as her mother-in-law and society led to hours of conversations with friends and family, but ultimately the significance of her family name won over. She moved her birth surname to her middle name and added his name as her last name.

Trying to please family—yours and his—can also disempower you from doing what is best for you.

According to Lauren Napolitano, a clinical psychologist specializing in therapy for couples and families in Philadelphia, when a child doesn't follow the tradition of taking a man's name, parents and grandparents may feel hurt.

"It can feel like a personal rejection of the parent rather than a cultivation of the child's identity," said Napolitano. "As parents, we tend to struggle with the perception that our children are extensions of us and not their own individuals, so when they do something that we would not choose or expect, we can feel hurt and rejected."

I conducted a mini poll asking people what "tradition" means to them. The results broke down like this:

- 41% said tradition is what my parents and grandparents did before me.
- 37% said tradition is what society expects me to do.
- 9% said tradition is a way to honor my husband and his family.
- 5% said tradition is the option that creates less friction.
- 4% said tradition is something tried and true, not trendy.
- 4% said tradition is a social agreement that acts like glue to keep a community together.

Those who are traditional are considered by our society to be upstanding citizens who don't push the boundaries or test authority. They do what's right, expected, predictable. They fall in line, not questioning whether the circumstance that established the tradition fits their individualism. Instead, they mold their thoughts and actions to fit the tradition.

Emily Fairchild, an associate director of undergraduate studies in the Department of Sociology at Harvard University, suggests that women may say it's romantic or traditional to take their husband's name because it is an easy answer—one that feels culturally safe—or because they haven't or don't want to think more deeply about it. The alternative of going with a nontraditional approach can feel risky, for both women and men. And then there's a whole other conversation about not even thinking about the options because then individuals can stay unaware of the gendered implications or resistant to challenging them.

Those who are considered untraditional often are described as radical, unique, flashy, or extreme.

But traditions are meant to evolve with society, and wedding traditions have been evolving for a long time.

"Wedding celebrations have become increasingly personalized and reflective of couples' values," explained Napolitano. "It's important that traditions evolve with societal beliefs because the partners getting married in 2025 are very different from partners getting married in 1960. Gender roles have evolved, relationship boundaries have shifted, and the strict adherence to customs and traditions has loosened over time."

Below are the origins of a few popular traditions and how they've evolved.

## Bridal Bouquet

In the Middle Ages, bouquets were packed with pungent herbs. Garlic, spices, and dill were classic choices meant to fend off evil spirits and bad luck that might plague the bride and wedding guests. The overpowering scents also helped mask the bride's body odor back when baths were not a daily (or even weekly) occurrence.

Now the bouquet is a symbol of beauty, love, and personal style, often reflecting the bride's taste and the overall wedding theme.

## First Look

Back when marriages were arranged as a business deal, the bride and groom weren't allowed to see or meet each other until they were at the altar. Parents of the bride feared that if the couple met before marrying, the groom might find the bride unattractive and would decide to call off the wedding. They were so careful, in fact, that part of the reason the bride wore a veil down the aisle was to prevent the groom from knowing what she looked like until the very last second—when it's too late to back out.

Today, couples often have a private "first look" to reveal their gown and tux. This intimate moment together helps calm the couple and allows them to connect in private.

## Bride's Parents Paying for Wedding

Back in the *olden days*, the father of the bride was obligated to cover the expenses of the wedding in exchange for the groom taking over the responsibility of his daughter. This practice came from the ancient concept of the wedding dowry, in which the family of the bride would pay the husband-to-be a sum of money as a sort of thanks for being willing to marry their daughter and become financially responsible for her.

This is no longer the hard-and-fast rule. Modern couples may pay for their own wedding, while parents of the bride and groom may give a set amount to the couple or forgo financing the wedding in lieu of helping pay off college debt or helping with a down payment on a house.

## Engagement Rings

Roman women wore rings of ivory, flint, bone, copper, and iron to signify a business contract or to affirm mutual love and obedience. It wasn't until 1850 that the engagement ring was given an official meaning. Pope Nicholas I declared that the engagement ring represented a man's intent to marry a woman, and gold was the most popular material for betrothal rings at the time. Diamond engagement rings didn't become popular until 1947, when the De Beers jewelry company launched an advertising campaign with the slogan "A diamond is forever."

## Taking the Husband's Name

The practice of a woman taking her husband's last name is a remnant of English common law called the doctrine of coverture, which we will explore more later in this book.

These traditions have morphed into what they are today, but the tradition of a wife taking her husband's last name really hasn't budged too much.

## Traditions Are Meant to Evolve

When my mom, Margie, married my dad, Carl, in 1959, she wore white gloves, a princess tiara with a veil, and layers of white petticoat crinolines and slips under her wedding dress skirt. At the end of the wedding reception, she said her mother removed her veil to symbolize the end of innocence and tied an apron around her waist to symbolize the beginning of wifely duties. My mom beamed describing her fond memory of proudly wearing the lacy apron with delicate flowers her mother handmade for her and becoming Mrs. Carl Swiger.

On hearing this tradition, my 30-year-old daughter was repulsed by what she considered a very sexist tradition. "What? That's awful!" she exclaimed. The thought that a woman's sole worth, purpose, and importance as a wife were to take care of her husband, children, and house was degrading to her and would not be part of her wedding.

The three of us laughed thinking about how times have changed.

Heather Farr, owner and senior wedding and event planner of Heather Farr Events in Milwaukee, agrees. "I think weddings should reflect the couple, not necessarily traditions. Historically, some traditions are tied to the transfer of the bride from her family to the groom . . . like the father giving the bride away. These do not feel right to today's modern couple. When couples redefine traditions, they create a world with more inclusivity and equality."

Brittany Bartz, owner and lead wedding planner of B-Rad Celebrations, based in New Berlin, Wisconsin, said the best question to ask is whether the bride and groom's wedding day is a representation of their personalities and their love. If the answer is yes, then you have a winning event on your hands, despite which traditions they did or didn't follow.

"I personally love that traditions evolve with time," said Bartz, who always asks her clients how to make their special day represent them. "This is a fun question to challenge the norm. For example, some couples don't like cake, so why should they cut a cake?"

There is no right or wrong answer when it comes to choosing a married name, but what is important is that the name reflects the couple and that they choose it together. If there are obstacles in your way that prevent you from empowering yourself to take the name you want—or keep the name you have—explore those obstacles and see whether you can move them out of your way.

## Exercise

Find a quiet place where you won't be disturbed and give yourself time and space to really feel the answers to these questions. If possible, instead of just reading the list, take the time to read each question, pause, and notice what reaction and feelings appear. Write them down so you can review them later. You may be surprised by how you really feel—happy, joyful, angry, anxious, light, obligated, annoyed, awkward, connected, empowered, scared, nervous, blissful, numb, giddy—but there is no right or wrong answer. This is all about you and your feelings. Are you ready?

- How do you feel about the last name you were given at birth?

______________________________________________

______________________________________________

- How do you feel when you think about taking your future husband's last name?

______________________________________________

______________________________________________

- How do you feel when you consider keeping your own last name?

______________________________________________

______________________________________________

- How do you feel when you consider hyphenating your name with your future husband's name?

______________________________________________

______________________________________________

- How do you feel when you consider another option, like changing your middle name to your maiden name and last name to his name, or adding his name to your last name so you have four names, or using your birth surname only professionally?

______________________________________________

______________________________________________

- How do you feel when you consider one of the above options but your husband changes his name too (changes his middle name to your maiden name or adds your name to his last name)?

__________________________________________________

__________________________________________________

- How do you feel when you think about your husband taking your last name?

__________________________________________________

__________________________________________________

- How do you feel when you consider giving your children your last name instead of your husband's last name if the two of you have different last names?

__________________________________________________

__________________________________________________

- How do you feel when you consider you and your husband both changing your last name to a new name that combines both of your last names together?

__________________________________________________

__________________________________________________

- How do you feel when you consider you and your husband both changing your last name to a new name that you create together that symbolizes your new relationship?

__________________________________________________

__________________________________________________

# *chapter four*
# SELF
*significance,*
*empowerment,*
# LEGACY,
*freedom*

Consider the legacy you wish to create with your name. Do you like your name? Do you want to create a new legacy? A surname legacy has so much wrapped into it—the story, the history, the culture. But here's the thing—yours is as important as, or equal to, any man's name.

## Alessandra and Stratton Sollevare

I talked to a woman whose family came up with an innovative, beautiful idea. When Alessandra married Stratton, she took his last name, but about a year into their marriage, they discussed the power of that decision going forward.

"We started reflecting on what we wanted our family to look like—what was our family culture," Alessandra said. She explained that on her husband's side, the culture was of vast disconnection, meaning it was okay to disown and not talk to members of the family, which was not okay with them. "We knew we wanted to change our name, but the question was, What do we change it to? Naming a child—that's easier than naming your entire family and their legacy."

She said they had the idea of taking a "name trip" to visit countries of their combined heritage to see whether one resonated more than another. They both had German ancestry, so they looked at German words. She is Italian, so they looked up Italian words like *radice*, meaning "roots," which reminded them of creating their own story. They also loved Iceland—all the nature, the feeling of being grounded, all the beauty—and hoped to be inspired.

"Nothing stuck," Alessandra said, "so we just put the intention out there that we wanted to change our name because family culture is very important to us, but we didn't push it."

Meanwhile, with the birth of each child, they felt remorse adding their current last name to the baby's birth certificate knowing it was going to change.

One day Alessandra was on a Zoom call. A woman on the call whom Alessandra had never met explained to the group that the night before, she woke up abruptly and out of nowhere this word revealed itself to her. It meant "lifting others up," or "to be a light"; the word was "sollevare" (soul-a-var-e-a). As soon as she heard it, Alessandra said she got chills all over her body.

"I think you just named our family," Alessandra wrote in the Zoom chat. "Just everything about it—obviously the meaning is really meaningful, but the word is really beautiful and it flows."

Once off the call, she found her husband and told him the story. He loved the name too. Over the next two years, they lived with the name while they filed all the paperwork. In March 2023, Alessandra gave birth to their fourth child, who was the first of their family to be given the Sollevare name. And in January 2024 the rest of the family finally had their court date to legally change their surnames as well.

"Names are so important to us—the meaning, the intention—and family is very important to us, so we wanted to be united in the legacy of who we really are," Alessandra said. "We don't want our kids to just accept, like, 'Well, this is just the way things are,' and not feel they have choices. We get to choose what's right for us, including our name."

## Jacqueline Beale-Delvecchio

Jacqueline Beale-Delvecchio had a similar thought for her kids.

"I love my hyphenated married name," she said. "It carries a lot of meaning for me. I'm curious, though, to see how my children handle it if they get married. We've always been clear that they can do whatever they want."

## Helen and James Kramer

In a *New York Times* article, Jason Kramer, 27, of Philadelphia, had parents who did the same thing. He explained the legacy his parents left him when they chose his last name.

"Part of their reasoning for taking a hyphenated last name was to make me and my brother think when we were getting married," said Kramer, a paralegal.

If it weren't for his parents, Kramer said, he probably would never have changed his name. But as they once told him, their decision to give him a hyphenated surname, Heitler-Klevans, was intended to encourage him to eventually consider alternate name options.

About a year before their 2020 wedding, he and his wife, Helen Kramer, sat down to discuss their choices, including the possibility of combining their last names. They decided that they would both take her name, in part because they liked the idea of passing it on to their future children.

"But if we hadn't gotten that push from my parents to have to think about it, then she would've just taken my name," Kramer said.

The couple's family and friends were complimentary about their decision, much to the pleasant surprise of the groom, who was expecting "some resistance," he said.

## Emily and Elías Hanno

In the same *New York Times* article, Elías Hanno, 34, of New Jersey, created a legacy of being the relative who set an example by taking his wife's name and encouraged open conversations.

Elías Hanno and his wife, Emily Hanno, don't consider themselves "unconventional" people, he said. When they decided that he would take her last name upon marriage, in 2018, their reason was practical. Her first name, Emily, is common, so she wanted a distinctive last name. Both halves of his original one, Sánchez-Eppler, felt too commonplace.

"The opportunity to challenge expectations has been one of the nicest ancillary benefits that wasn't really part of the decision-making process," said Hanno, a manager at Schmidt Futures.

The couple especially liked informing their youngest family members of the choice. "Our niece and nephew are growing up thinking that it's totally normal for a man to take a woman's name, and they'll expect to have open conversations on what they want to do when they find a partner, which is really sweet and exciting," he said.

It hasn't all been smooth going, however. Some relatives have expressed displeasure at not having their family name continue, and Elías, who is Hispanic, said he needed to be "a little more intentional about marking that identity in other ways."

## Davina Newcomb

Davina Newcomb decided to name herself. "I was fine with my maiden name, Taylor. It was pretty middle of the road. After getting married, I became a Mitchell, which was also pretty common. When I divorced, I decided to try something completely new. I took my new surname from my favorite book series, Newcomb. So I like my current name quite a bit."

## Unintentional Legacy

Sometimes the legacy you create is an accident or mistake, but it can surely make for a fun story.

When my second son was born, I incorrectly spelled his middle name on the birth certificate. I transposed the *a* and *e* in Michael, so his middle name is spelled Micheal.

I didn't realize I misspelled the name until someone pointed out to me that he had an unusual spelling of Michael. I was embarrassed and ashamed, so I just giggled and agreed.

I kept the mistake a secret from my son and the rest of the family. They often teased me about my horrible spelling habits when I'd handwrite captions in scrapbooks and include notes in cards or letters. I didn't want to admit my poor grammar left a permanent stain on my child's name.

I've since realized I have dyslexia, which explains the difficulty I had reading and spelling. Often my words come out mixed up, like "My hairs are leggy" instead of "My legs are hairy" or "The goat had a bo and a duck" instead of "The goat had a doe and a buck." Somewhere between my brain and mouth, things all get jumbled up and come out wonky.

When my son was in college, he noticed my shameful mistake on his birth certificate. But instead of being upset, he embraced it. He's gone on to be an artist and incorporates the uniqueness of his name as his identity.

To add to the irony, it turns out "Micheal" is a common Irish spelling and pronunciation of the name "Michael." Not only have I learned to laugh at my mistakes and accept my "imperfections" but also I trust that sometimes things were meant to be, even if unintended.

## Kathleen Heneghan

Kathleen Heneghan had a similar situation. She said she loved the significance of her birth surname and wanted to pass it on to her children, but a clerical error created a lot of work for her as well as a family tale that has become part of her legacy.

"I love my birth family name," she said. "I like the fact that Heneghans come from a specific area in Ireland, and I was raised with a strong ethnic identification. My parents listened to Irish radio on Saturday mornings and took us to Irish dance lessons. All my grandparents emigrated from Ireland, and I like the fact that my first name and last name make sense together."

She went on to say, "I have an aunt whose name is also Kathleen, and as a child it bothered me that she changed her last name and took her husband's Polish last name. I told myself then that I wouldn't change my last name. Sometimes I wonder if my husband had an Irish last name or a less ethnic (Polish) name if I would have considered taking his surname. I don't think I would have, but I do wonder."

Kathleen said she and her husband gave both their kids a first name, a middle name, her last name, and then her husband's last name. "I just wanted to get my name in there and envisioned it like this: Jacob Louis-Heneghan Narowski, or on forms, Jacob L. H. Narowski [both kids do use the double initials as their middle name].

"All seemed fine, until I went to register Jacob for kindergarten and realized that I didn't have his birth certificate," Kathleen said. "I went to the records office at city hall to get it, but they couldn't find it. I said, 'Well, look under Heneghan,' and they found it. The hyphen was in the wrong place, although his Social Security card was correct. Okay, so the last name was hyphenated incorrectly and cut off. It read Heneghan-Narows. Bleh. My daughter's birth certificate was correct."

Kathleen continued. "So, 'Get Jacob's birth certificate corrected' was on my list of things to do for 10 years. Finally, when he was 15, I got around to doing it because I was motivated that his driver's license and tax records would be correct once he got a job.

"I figured that I would need to complete and send in the paperwork. Nope. We needed to hire a lawyer and go to court in front of a judge to get his name legally changed. It was interesting and fun, and the judge was awesome. He was an alumni from Jacob's high school and sang the school fight song for Jacob. It was amusing, and all resolved in the end. But what a pain for a clerical error.

"Sometimes we call him Heneghan-Narows just for fun. On his college diploma he had all four of his names spelled out individually."

## Unfortunate Names

Some women feel obligated to take their husband's name as a symbol of love, honor, and respect. And again, there is no right or wrong answer—simply choices. But when a man has, let's say, an "unfortunate" family name, like Assman, Damm, or Cockburn, is that really the legacy you want to carry with you the rest of your life and pass on to your children? Isn't the world tough enough without giving kids a name that screams "please bully me"?

So many women say things like, "But it means so much to him," or "I want my in-laws to like me," or "I want the whole romantic package including taking his name," but if his name is something like Pitstick, Death, or Grossweiner, I implore you to ask your fiancé to debunk tradition and take your name.

Do you need some encouragement? Channel the lyrics from the Beyoncé song, "Formation": "You know you that b**ch when you cause all this conversation."

Remember, you have choices, and so does he. The discussion doesn't have to be heavy and drawn out. Try popping the question in along with your daily check-in. "How was your day? Did you Venmo your mother? Would you take my last name?"

I came across a Twitter post from someone with the last name of Medick asking whether anyone else had problems with their offensive last names. These are great examples of the importance of choice and the option of taking the bride's name.

- As a person named James Butts, I know these problems.
- Paul Gay said, "I was trying to get insurance, but when I filled in my last name, I got an error message—Word Not Allowed. You have entered a profanity or a not allowed word, please change it."
- Scott wrote, "When I got my computer, I had to set my last name as 'Spron' because Sporn contains offensive language."
- Ted Cummings said, "Trust me, it's a club. It doesn't help that I graduated from Seaman High School."
- "As a Dickman, I know the struggle is real."
- "With the last name Dicks, I have to remind people to check their spam folder more often than a Nigerian prince."

## Name Children after Mother

"I feel like my family history is just as important as my husband's," said Shauna Kase. "My family is so much in our lives, and the way I grew up is much more present in how I raise my children. I gave my second born my maiden name as a first name, so it is very well talked about what my last name used to be. I still feel strongly attached to that name."

One woman told me, "We both kept our names when we got married, but my husband hyphenated my last name onto his when our daughter was born because we gave her my last name."

In a Bravo interview, the *Vanderpump Rules* boss, Lisa Vanderpump, shares her decision to keep her name. Lisa married her husband, Ken Todd, back in 1982, and their relationship is going strong, but fans still ask about her married name decision.

"Ken had already been married before ... but I felt that 'Vanderpump' was a much nicer name than 'Todd,' sorry, no disrespect to my husband," she shared, adding that because Ken's ex-wife kept the name Todd, she didn't want to follow suit.

"I never actually changed my name," she said. "I didn't change my passport. I didn't change anything. So I was always Lisa Vanderpump," she explained in the interview, noting that their two children, Pandora and Max, have both their names, as Vanderpump-Todd.

The legacy of giving a child the mother's birth surname isn't a new trend. In the late nineteenth century, it was customary to give children, especially the eldest son, a first name that honored the mother's family, especially if the mother's family was of high standing.

In 1855, Caroline and Julius Morton gave birth to their first son and named him Joy, which was his mother's birth surname. He went on to be an American businessman and entrepreneur best known for founding Morton Salt and establishing the Morton Arboretum in Lisle, Illinois.

Franklin Delano Roosevelt, the thirty-second US president, born on January 30, 1882, was given his mother's birth surname as his middle name. His parents, businessman James Roosevelt I and Sara Ann Delano of Hyde Park, New York, came from wealthy, established New York families—the Roosevelts, the Aspinwalls, and the Delanos, respectively.

In 1892, Benjamin and Fannie Holland gave birth to a son and named him Spessard, his mother's birth surname. Spessard Holland went on to be a governor of Florida and a US senator for Florida.

George Herbert Walker Bush, the forty-first US president, born on June 12, 1924, was also given his mother's birth surname. His parents, Prescott Bush and Dorothy Walker Bush, were both descendants of wealthy parents.

## Matrilineal

In addition to the wealthy, there are a few societies around the world today that are considered matrilineal, where inheritance and lineage are traced through the mother's line.

**Indonesia:** The Minangkabau people of West Sumatra are the largest-known matrilineal society, with approximately 4.2 million members. Ownership of a family's property—their homes, rice paddies, and the like—passes from mother to daughter. While Minangkabau women's roles are what Americans consider conventional—they take care of the children and home—their sense of equality with men and their shared power are not.

Both genders say that they value each other and their roles equally. When couples marry, husbands move into their wives' homes, nearly all decisions require consensus between men and women, and, significantly, girls are treasured.

**India:** The Khasi people of Meghalaya, in northeast India, are another example of a matrilineal society. Also the Nairs, a Hindu community primarily found in the state of Kerala, India, are matrilineal.

A Khasi husband typically moves into his wife's home, and both wife and husband participate equally in raising their children. Children receive their mother's last name, and the youngest daughter inherits the ancestral property.

**China:** The Mosuo people, living in the Himalayan foothills, also practice a matrilineal system. Women are often the head of the house, inheritance is through the female line, and women make the business decisions.

When a Mosuo woman or man expresses interest in a potential partner, it is the woman who gives the man permission to visit her. They call it a "walking marriage" because the man comes over only after dark, if he has permission, and leaves before sunrise. After the birth of a child, the man has no moral, cultural, or legal obligation to take care of the child.

The support from the woman's extended family allows both the man and woman to engage in sexual relations with whomever they please. Divorce is never an issue because the man and woman are not legally bound together, thus sharing very few of the same responsibilities. There are also never any disputes over who owns custody of the child since the child belongs to the mother's extended family and takes the mother's last name.

**Costa Rica:** The Bribri people in eastern Costa Rica and northern Panama are matrilineal. Tribal lineage is passed down through the mother, and knowledge and tradition are passed down by the grandmother because women are revered as the heirs of life.

This culture is committed to live out the matriarchal vision in alignment with the Earth Mother. Therefore, land is handed down from the mother to her children, and the only people who can prepare the sacred cacao drink for their religious rituals are women. The women create entrepreneurial endeavors around ecotourism ventures, organic agriculture, crafts, food and traditional beverages, and educational opportunities.

**North America:** Several Native North American groups, such as the Cherokee, Choctaw, and Haida, also practice matrilineal descent. Also the Haudenosaunee (Six Nations) of North America honor matrilineal lines.

## Patrilineal

But passing on the father's name is still the norm in the US. In 2002, researchers found that about 97% of married couples passed down only the father's last name to their children. Fifteen years later, that number remained the same. According to a 2017 paper, heterosexual parents adopting children found that parents gave their child only the father's last name 96% of the time.

One of the reasons for passing on the father's name is due to a law based on the concept of "bastard inheritance." It originated from English law and existed in the US until the 1969 Family Reform Act, which allowed a "bastard," a child born out of wedlock, to inherit from parents through wills and other legal documents, not just by name.

Initially, to prove a male child had a direct lineage to the father and was the rightful heir to his inheritance, the child had to have the same last name as the father. Without the father's name, the male heir was considered illegitimate. The only way for the child to get the father's name was for the mother to be married to the father, or at least say he was the father. Although the concept of using the father's name to legitimize a child is now a moot point since lineage can be proven for a child through DNA, the tradition of giving the child the father's surname continues.

I asked a man who was 91 at the time, if he were to have children in today's social climate, would it bother him to give his children his wife's last name. He told me that as long as his son had his name, he wouldn't mind if his daughter had his wife's name.

*The Atlantic* published an article entitled "A Patriarchal Tradition That Just Won't Budge," which states that women today aren't legally mandated to give their husband's last name to their children but US bureaucracy has continued to enforce patrilineal naming conventions.

The article mentions Doborah Anthony, a professor of legal studies at the University of Illinois at Springfield, who after researching court cases in which couples battled over who had the right to pass down the surname to their kids found that "the mother almost always lost." Anthony explained that judges have repeatedly used the legal doctrine of the "best interests of the child" to side with the father.

"There's this implicit understanding that having the father's last name is inherently in the child's best interest," she said, citing cases where judges argued that taking the father's surname would deepen the family relationship or provide children with more financial security later in life. Some states, such as Louisiana, maintain policies that enforce patrilineal surnaming as a default when the father is known and supports the children, unless both partners agree otherwise.

Cheryl Nieber, a licensed clinical social worker, has this to say about married name choices:

> The long-standing tradition of a woman taking a man's name when married is steeped in patriarchy—ugh. There are numerous historical contexts for why women were expected (or forced) to take a man's name when getting married, but they all have the same patriarchal foundation. The gist is that the man is superior to the woman, he completes her, her identity is to merge with his, or that his family now owns her—I mean, it's bleak.
>
> For some women, the historical context of taking your husband's name provides enough reason to simply say, no thank you, and retain her maiden name. For others, this is just one deciding factor in a much more complex decision. Even if they don't love the patriarchal steeped tradition, for some modern brides, the benefits outweigh the ick factor. Afterall, if you have always hated your last name, this could be a great time to change it (I see you Hofecker).
>
> A deeply progressive and feminist friend of mine hated the historical context of "taking your husband's last name" as a tradition. She was raised Jewish, but her last name was, well, not Jewish sounding at all. When she and her husband married, it was an easy decision for her. His last name was stereotypically Jewish, and she loved that! Despite name inequity's patriarchal roots, she made the choice to take his name because it was what she wanted. Talk about empowering!

Another woman, Shelia, told me that she didn't change her name at marriage because she always wanted to keep her birth surname and since she didn't get married until age 38, "I was like, why bother?" Although her husband was disappointed, he said he would respect her decision.

Feeling a little guilty, and empowered to make the decision on her own, she decided for their first wedding anniversary to secretly add his last name to her surname. Since the traditional gift for a one-year anniversary is paper, she surprised her husband by framing the letter from the Social Security Administration office.

Unfortunately, she didn't get the response she expected.

"I was upset when he was like, whatever, since you didn't do it right away."

Who wouldn't blame her for being upset after putting so much thought and effort into this romantic gesture only to have her spouse dismiss the gift? A name-change is a lifelong, permanent decision. Why would he trivialize such an intimate act on a momentous occasion for newlyweds?

Is it possible his masculinity was wrapped up in his friends and family witnessing his bride publicly take his name? Was it important to him that they shared a last name, or was it more about wanting her to succumb to the way he felt it should be done? Was he withholding his love and affection as punishment for her not following tradition?

Wouldn't it be interesting to know? Most men aren't vulnerable enough to answer honestly. And most women don't feel they have the right to ask.

Crushed and hurt, Shelia called the SSA to ask whether she could remove the name she added, but the clerk told her she'd have to pay a fee and fill out all the paperwork again. Discouraged, she left it the way it was.

"When I explained my situation to the lady at the SSA office, she sympathized with me and suggested I be sure to request a name change if there is a divorce decree," Shelia said nonchalantly, laughing it off as if to say, "What are you going to do?

## Exercise

Take a few minutes to reflect on these questions. Your first response is always the best. Be aware of your initial thoughts and physical reactions. After you finish all the questions, go back and consider whether there are any beliefs you want to change.

- How do you feel about your name? What is the legacy or story behind it?

- Do you want to create a new legacy? What story do you want to tell about your name in the future?

- If you don't take his name, does it mean you love, honor, and cherish him any less?

- In terms of gender equality, does the same hold true for women? If a man takes his wife's name, would that gesture show he loves, honors, and cherishes her even more?

- If he doesn't change his name, does it diminish how much he loves, honors, and cherishes her?

- When a man says "I've waited all my life to find the one person I want to give my name to," what feelings does that invoke?

- If you said to your fiancé, "I love you and want to give you my name," what do you think his response would be?

- How have you romanticized the gesture of taking your husband's last name?

- Honoring your husband and your husband honoring you is a mutual respect and love for each other. With that information in mind, let's consider this question again. Can you love, honor, and cherish your husband, and keep your last name, or hyphenate your names, or have your name as the family last name?

# *chapter five*

# SELF

*significance,*

*empowerment,*

*legacy,*

# FREEDOM

Enjoy the freedom to choose what feels right for you. We're lucky in the United States. We get to choose whatever name fits our situation: take his name, take her name, hyphenate names, create a new name. There is no right or wrong, and there are so many choices. Consider what's most important and have intentional conversations; choose the name that best fits you and your partner. I assure you that any name option you can possibly imagine has already been done. The question is, if you and your spouse could do anything you wanted with your name when you marry, what would you wish it to be?

## Alexa and Carlos PenaVega

When the *Spy Kids* star Alexa Vega and Nickelodeon alum Carlos Pena got married in 2014, they decided to combine their last names.

"When we got married, we realized that we wanted to start fresh," Alexa said in a recent *E! News* interview. "We wanted to start a new generation of something. So we became the PenaVegas."

On a podcast, Carlos agreed that they always loved the idea of making their name PenaVega, but they thought they'd have to hire an attorney and go through the whole court process.

"Honestly, we didn't know if [combining our names] was even possible," Alexa said. "But we went into the courthouse and were signing all the paperwork, and they're like, 'OK, so who's taking whose last name? What's happening?'"

They weren't sure whether simply writing their new combined name on their marriage certificate would make it legal, but they decided to give it a try.

"We looked at each other, and we just wrote it down," she said, "not knowing if it would work, because there was no hyphen, nothing. We just made it one word."

Carlos said once they had the "stamp of approval" on their official marriage certificate, they updated everything, including their Social Security cards, driver's license, and passports.

The couple now has three children—sons Ocean and Kingston and daughter Rio—and a YouTube channel called *La Vida PenaVega*.

## Darcy and Jeff Ward

Darcy Ward and Jeff Conley left their name change decision up to chance.

"We didn't want to start our marriage with the patriarchal assumption that I would give up my name," explained Darcy, who is a nurse and certified nurse-midwife in Ann Arbor, Michigan. "However, I wanted to have the same last name as my future kids, and Jeff and I felt that hyphenation wasn't a generationally sustainable option."

Before their 2019 wedding, the couple considered creating a new name but felt that it was an unnecessary hassle to both go through the name-change process. Their solution was to flip a coin at the altar.

"We were talking about what would be 'fair' or 'equal,' and that's what caused me to suggest flipping a coin," explained Jeff, an economist. "The expected outcome of the toss was the same for both names. We were both comfortable with either possible outcome and with deviating from established wedding norms."

At the end of the ceremony, before the couple walked down the aisle together, Darcy's brother explained what was about to happen, and then the best man flipped a brass coin engraved with Darcy's and Jeff's surnames and profiles. When the coin landed with Darcy's side up, people said she won, but Jeff saw it a different way.

"People said I won," Darcy said. "But Jeff was quick to point out that he was the one who got something new, so in that sense he won. Aww, right? I would highly recommend the flip, but only if you're truly okay with it going either way. There are plenty of ways to make the right decision, and we had a lot of fun making the right one for us."

When I talked to the couple five years after they got hitched, Jeff added, "I hope everyone feels fulfilled by how they're known after they're married. I don't have any regrets. The flip fulfilled our needs, and I consider changing my last name to be more meaningful than the alternative. So I'm really glad things turned out the way they did and that now we are a family of three under the same Ward banner."

Darcy and Jeff started a new trend in 2019. Today on TikTok, it's more common to see couples flip a coin at the altar, or play three rounds of "rock, paper, scissors" to determine whether to take the bride or groom's surname. Other current trends include allowing the wedding guests to vote for the winning surname or having random strangers on TikTok determine "who has the cooler surname" between the two people getting married.

## Jayne and Sam Falcon

When Sam Gonzalez proposed to Jayne Falcon, he asked for not only her hand in marriage but also her name.

"Growing up, I loved the movie *The Maltese Falcon*," Sam explained, referring to the 1941 film starring Humphrey Bogart as private investigator Sam Spade. "The main character has the same first name as mine, and when I fell in love with Jayne, I thought it would be so cool to change my name and be Sam Falcon."

Jayne said Sam, a paramedic, introduced her to the movie when they were dating and teased her that he was going to take her name, but it wasn't a serious conversation until the Illinois couple was engaged.

"It felt good when he asked if he could change his name to mine," said Jayne. "I've kind of made a name for myself in my line of work as a paramedic and firefighter, so I was glad to keep it. And I love that Sam took my name so we could share it together."

Americans haven't always had the freedom to choose his or hers or to create a new name. It was the law—until relatively recently—that a woman had to take her husband's surname. In some other countries, there are still laws around what women and men can do with their last names when they marry.

## Coverture

Women and men did not always have the option to choose their own legacy through their names. Let's back up a little and talk about where our modern Western idea of a wife taking her husband's surname began.

Way back around 1000–1500 CE, England used a system of common law. Rules and traditions weren't written down in one place. Instead, these laws were developed over time through court decisions and were eventually recognized as English common law. It was under this system that the doctrine of coverture that we discussed earlier developed.

Basically, it asserted that once married, a woman's identity was "covered" by her husband. From the moment of her marriage, a woman was known as a *femme covert*, or covered woman; she and her husband essentially became one. With their identity basically erased under this law, women could not own property or enter into contracts on their own. Husbands had complete control over their wives, legally and financially.

Coverture laws were designed to protect a woman—she was "covered" by her father until marriage and then "covered" by her husband. A married woman's legal existence was considered merged with her husband's, so she could not be sued or punished separately because the couple was considered one person. That person was the husband, so when she married, she dropped her father's name and took her husband's surname.

As England invaded and colonized territories across the globe, including what is now the United States, Canada, Australia, India, and parts of Africa, it also spread its legal systems, including the doctrine of coverture.

In March 1776, Abigail Adams wrote a letter to her husband, John Adams, which is now part of a collection at the Massachusetts Historical Society. At the time, her husband was a member of the Continental Congress, which drafted the Articles of Confederation, later serving as the first Constitution of the United States. She was hoping for relief from coverture:

> In the new Code of Laws which I suppose it will be necessary for you to make, I desire you would Remember the Ladies, and be more generous and favorable to them than your ancestors. Do not put such unlimited power into the hands of the Husbands. Remember all Men would be tyrants if they could. If particular care and attention

> is not paid to the Ladies we are determined to foment a Rebellion, and will not hold ourselves bound by any Laws in which we have no voice, or Representation.

In the New York Historical, "Women and the American Story," the modern summary of the response from John Adams basically said:

> Your letter is the first time I heard that women are planning to rebel too. I'm being very rude, but your letter was so saucy I won't cross it out. We know better than to give women more power. You know men aren't really in charge, even if the law says so. We have to follow what women say already. If women try to fight for more equality, I hope George Washington and the army would fight back. Every politician would too.

Below is Abigail's response. She sounds a bit annoyed. What do you think?

> I cannot say that I think you very generous to the ladies, for whilst you are proclaiming peace and good will to men, emancipating all nations, you insist upon retaining an absolute power over wives. But you must remember that arbitrary power is like most other things which are very hard, very liable to be broken—and notwithstanding all your wise laws and maxims we have it in our power not only to free ourselves but to subdue our masters, and without violence throw both your natural and legal authority at our feet.

And so the fight to abolish the doctrine of coverture began, but it was very slow—more than 200 years in the making.

There was some help along the way. Before Theodore Roosevelt became president in 1901, he advocated for women's rights in his Harvard undergraduate thesis, titled "The Practicability of Equalizing Men and Women before the Law." He wrote:

> Viewed purely in the abstract, I think there can be no question that women should have equal rights as men . . . Especially as regards the laws relating to marriage, there should be the most absolute equality between the two sexes. I do not think the woman should assume the man's name.

Women could not choose their legacy while coverture existed. Even today, there are still ghosts of coverture floating around us.

## History of Married Names in the US

It wasn't until 1982 that all 50 US states allowed women to keep their birth surname when getting married.

A lawyer in Montgomery, Alabama, Patrick Mahaney, explained it this way:

> It was formerly the law of the state of Alabama that a married woman automatically took the last name of the husband upon entering marriage. This was the common law of Alabama for many years. However, in the case of *State v. Taylor*, 415 So. 2d 1043 (Ala. 1982) the Alabama Supreme Court held, under "equal protection" grounds, that the wife was authorized, but not required to assume the name of the husband. The common law of England held that when a woman on her marriage assumes the

> surname of her husband in substitution for her father's name, she acquires a new name by repute; the change of name is in fact, rather than by law, in consequence of marriage. But a woman is not required to do so and may continue to use her previous name.

This freedom for women came almost 130 years after Lucy Stone was credited in 1855 with being the first woman in the US to keep her birth surname after marriage.

Lucy, born in August 1818, was a prominent US orator, abolitionist, and suffragist and a vocal advocate and organizer promoting rights for women. In 1847, Stone became the first woman from Massachusetts to earn a college degree. She spoke out for women's rights and against slavery.

The man she married, Henry Browne Blackwell, was born in May 1825 and was an advocate for social and economic reform. He was one of the founders of the American Woman Suffrage Association and the Republican Party, which was created in 1854 to combat the expansion of slavery into the western territories. Later, after their marriage, they published *The Woman's Journal*, starting in 1870 in Boston, Massachusetts.

Henry first saw Lucy giving a speech—later known as her "Fugitive Mother" speech—at an antislavery meeting in New York in May 1853. After courting, Henry proposed marriage to Lucy, but she rejected Henry's proposition. She knew marriage would require her to surrender control over herself and would prevent her from pursuing her chosen work.

Back in the 1850s, the US still enforced the laws of coverture—the legal doctrine stating that upon marriage, a woman had no legal existence apart from her husband. Her rights and obligations would be incorporated under his, so she could not own property, enter into contracts, or control the money she earned, among other things.

Henry, determined to convince Lucy that his belief in marriage wouldn't require her to sacrifice her individuality or career, reasoned that a marriage based on equality would enable each of them to accomplish more than they could alone.

After years of pursuing her, Henry won Lucy over by personifying the belief that couples could shape their own marriages, regardless of society's laws.

In their wedding vows, they dropped the word "obey," and Blackwell declared that he stood for equal marriage, listing the laws that did not recognize women as independent beings.

Lucy continued to sign correspondence as "Lucy Stone" or "Lucy Stone (only)," but when she tried to register a deed for property she purchased in Wisconsin, the registrar insisted she sign it as "Lucy Stone Blackwell."

Lucy consulted prominent lawyers, including Salmon Chase, who later became chief justice of the United States, to verify there was nothing illegal about keeping her name intact. When she received confirmation, Lucy Stone made a public announcement at the May 7, 1856, convention of the American Anti-Slavery Society in Boston that her name remained Lucy Stone.

While Lucy Stone's decision was a landmark moment, it wasn't a common practice for other women, mainly because of deeply ingrained cultural and legal traditions, social pressure, and the perception of marriage as a union where women's identities were subsumed under their husbands'. The movement for women to keep their birth surname was slow to catch on until the 1970s, when a wave of feminism swept the country.

According to Marcia K. Morgan, PhD, a national expert on gender issues, legal reforms were important to achieve equity between the sexes.

In her book *Should I Change My Name*, Morgan wrote:

> During this second wave of feminism in the 1970s, women continued fighting against states that still had laws not allowing women to keep their birth surnames. Many of

> these women trailblazers, including Ruth Bader Ginsburg, helped pass laws around access to voting, bank loans, credit, getting passports, and other roadblocks based on retaining their own names.

Ask your grandmother or a woman who asserted any independence in the 1970s to share a story of gender inequality. I'm sure she'll have at least one.

One woman told me she kept her birth surname when she got married in 1972. She and her husband were both young college graduates protesting the Vietnam War and racial injustices and supporting women's rights. They both liked the idea of pushing back against the patriarchal tradition by having her keep her birth surname.

Upon hearing of her nuptials, her employer took it upon himself to make her paycheck payable to Mrs. Alan Whiteburg, assuming that was her married name. She promptly informed the owner of the dental office she managed that her legal name had not changed. But her next paycheck was again made out to Mrs. Alan Whiteburg.

"When clients were at my desk, he would make judgmental comments knowing full well I could hear them," she recalls. "He would make offhand remarks about radical feminists who don't take their husband's name and how he would never hire someone like that. I didn't want to lose my job, so I just kept quiet and accepted my paycheck with the name he wanted to use."

While it was not legally permissible for employers to outright refuse to pay married women using their birth surname in 1972, it was a common and often successful form of gender discrimination. Employers frequently pressured women to change their names, and some state laws at the time supported the practice by making it difficult for women to use their birth names on official documents.

The 1970s may seem like a long time ago, but there are still parents, grandparents, and lawmakers who grew up with these social norms, which still influence what they believe is right and wrong today.

Morgan reminds us that in the 1970s, "Women were living and breathing coverture's oppression in their lives." Here are a few other changes from the 1970s.

- 1971: The US Supreme Court rules in *Phillips v. Martin Marietta Corp.* that under Title VII of the Civil Rights Act of 1964, an employer may not, in the absence of business necessity, refuse to hire women with preschool-age children while hiring men with such children.
- 1972: Title IX of the Education Amendments prohibits sex discrimination in all aspects of education programs that receive federal support.
- 1972: The US Supreme Court rules in *Eisenstadt v. Baird* that a Massachusetts law criminalizing the distribution of contraceptives to unmarried persons for the purpose of preventing pregnancy violated the right to equal protection.
- 1973: The US Supreme Court declares that the Constitution protects women's right to terminate an early pregnancy, thus making abortion legal (*Roe v. Wade*). Note: this was overturned in 2022.
- 1974: The US Supreme Court rules in *Cleveland Board of Education v. LaFleur* that overly restrictive maternity leave regulations in public schools violate the Due Process Clause of the Fifth and Fourteenth Amendments, which makes it illegal to force pregnant women to take maternity leave on the assumption that they are incapable of working in their physical condition.
- 1974: The Equal Credit Opportunity Act is enacted by the US Congress and signed into law by President Gerald Ford, allowing

unmarried women to get a credit card and/or a mortgage in their own name with or without a husband.

- 1975: The US Supreme Court rules in *Taylor v. Louisiana* that excluding women from jury service solely based on their sex violates the Sixth Amendment right to a fair trial.
- 1975: The US Supreme Court strikes down a Tennessee law that required a woman to change her name to her husband's name before she could register to vote.
- 1978: The Pregnancy Discrimination Act makes it illegal for employers to discriminate against pregnant women.
- 1979: Louisiana becomes the last state in the US to strike down its "Head and Master" marriage law, which permitted a husband to have final say regarding all household decisions and jointly owned property without his wife's knowledge or consent.

1972 also saw the first issue of *Ms.* magazine, the first American feminist magazine, cofounded by journalist and social/political activist Gloria Steinem along with founding editors Letty Cottin Pogrebin, Mary Thom, Patricia Carbine, Joanne Edgar, Nina Finkelstein, Mary Peacock, and Margaret Sloan-Hunter. This revolutionary publication aimed to provide modern feminist news and information and popularized the prefix Ms. as an alternative to Miss and Mrs.

Unlike males whose honorific went from Master to Mr. when they turned 18, the correct etiquette to address females was tied to their marital status. Women went from Miss to Mrs. upon marriage no matter what their age, so an unmarried woman in her seventies would still be titled Miss Sue Smith, for example.

Although the custom of prefixes has relaxed, historically, "Mrs." translated to "the wife of," so it was always followed by the husband's first and last name. You would be publicly shamed if you addressed a married woman as Mrs. Jane Doe, because she is not "the wife of" Jane Doe. Technically, the correct usage is Mrs. John Doe, even if she kept her birth surname after marriage.

With the popularity of women keeping their birth surnames upon marriage in the 1970s, a new prefix—Ms.—was necessary, but the outdated traditions still linger today.

I was appalled when I registered my 3-year-old twin grandkids as guests on my Walt Disney World Resort registration. The form had a required "prefix" field for adults and children. To register my grandchildren, I had to choose from the dropdown list, which consisted of Mr., Mrs., Ms., Mstr., Miss, Dr., or Mx. In my opinion, no one should be addressed as Master, especially not a boy under the age of 18. As a tiny bit of rebellion, I chose "Mx." for all of us.

Another ghost of coverture was only recently extinguished in 2005, thanks to the evolving social acceptance of same-sex marriages. The use of "spinster" and "bachelor" to identify unmarried individuals was removed from mortgage documents to accommodate same-sex couples and because the terms were (finally) considered outdated and potentially demeaning. They were replaced with the non-gender-specific "single" or "unmarried."

An article titled "It's Time to Break Chains of 'Spinster,'" originally published in 1994 by the *Chicago Tribune*, states, "The word [spinster] rankles women all the more on mortgage forms because at the very moment they are committing the liberating act of buying a place of their own, they find themselves transported back to a time when society defined a woman's worth primarily by her relation to men and marriage, a time when it was assumed that the unmarried woman was the unfulfilled woman."

One woman told me, "As I refinanced my home again, I remembered the word 'spinster' on the paperwork. At that moment, I realized I was still pinned down by the stereotypes of the society that implemented it. But only pinned down by the words because I will constantly define my own identity."

## Laws of Other Countries

Some other countries have laws around what couples can and can't do with their surnames when they marry.

**Japan:** A married couple must have the same last name. It can be his name or her name, but it must be the same (96% of married Japanese women take their husband's surname). No hyphenating, no creating a new name, and women cannot keep their birth surname unless her husband changes his surname. In fact, the law does not recognize married couples who have different surnames as lawful husband and wife.

**France:** Law dictates that individuals retain the surname listed on their birth certificate, regardless of marital status. Married individuals in France can choose to use their spouse's surname as a *nom d'usage*, or "usage name," for everyday purposes—such as on bank statements or in social settings. However, for official documents, such as passports or driver's licenses, individuals must retain their birth surname.

**Quebec:** Since 1981, provincial law in Quebec has forbidden a woman from taking her husband's surname after marriage. In fact, each spouse must retain their name during the marriage and exercise their civil rights under that name. Prior to the reform of the civil code, women's last names were automatically changed to their husband's surname when they got married. The law was created to protect a woman's identity and prevent the societal pressure to change names upon marriage, which is seen as a step toward gender equality.

**Greece:** In 1983 Greece adopted a new marriage law that guaranteed gender equality between the spouses. Since then, women are required to keep their birth surnames when they get married.

**Italy:** Spouses keep their original surnames. According to the Italian civil code, a woman who marries keeps her surname and has the option of adding her husband's surname after hers.

**Turkey:** Since 2014, women are allowed to keep their birth surnames. Previously, the Turkish civil code required a married woman to use her husband's surname or add her husband's name after her name by applying to the civil registry office. In 2014, the constitutional court ruled that prohibiting married women from keeping their birth surname was a violation of their rights.

**South Africa:** Previously, the law did not allow men to take their wife's surname. They needed to apply to the director-general for permission, which was not always granted. But in September 2024, a free state high court ruling allowed two husbands to adopt their wives' surnames, arguing the Registration of Births and Deaths Act unfairly discriminated on the basis of sex/gender. The high court held that the provision of the law perpetuated archaic gender roles and constituted unfair discrimination against men, and it granted the relief sought by the applicants.

**Iceland:** There is no use of family names in this Nordic nation. Instead, it uses a patronymic or matronymic naming convention based on a parent's first name—typically the father's but sometimes the mother's. For example, if a man named Jón has a son named Magnús, the son's full name would be Magnús Jónsson. The suffix "-son" literally means "son of." If Jón had a daughter, her full name would be Anna Jónsdóttir—the suffix "-dóttir" meaning "daughter of." In recent years, there has been a rise in the use of matronymics, and this shift reflects Iceland's broader focus on gender equality. In 2019, the Icelandic parliament passed the Gender Autonomy Act, allowing nonbinary individuals to use the gender-neutral suffix "-bur," meaning "child," so Magnús or Anna's last name could be Jónsbur.

## Married Name Options

I asked my "friends" on Facebook what they did with their last names. Their responses were as unique and personalized as each friend.

Kate Moore Lauderbaugh: "I kept my maiden name as my middle name. But my license for some reason has my middle initial of my old middle name. So now I have to use that if I want anything to match my license."

MaryKim Whiteside: "I had every intention of switching to my new married name but panicked at the DMV. It took two years to switch everything from my old married name back to my maiden name. So in a moment of sheer panic, I hyphenated."

Maria Lyn Pearcy Boynton: "I simply added my husband's last name to my name without a hyphen. The kids have our shared name. It was important to me that we had a team name, as it were, which I know is a personal preference."

Kathleen Heneghan: "My kids have my name as part of their middle names and my husband's name as their legal last names. A friend mentioned just adding the husband's surname casually and avoiding the legal name change. I thought that was a good idea and kind of what I do. You can refer to yourself however you want on social media or a return address label, or usually choose how you want people to address you at work, right? Such a good idea! In school situations with my kids, I would sometimes introduce myself as Kathleen Heneghan Narowski just to let on that those Narowski kids were mine."

Jacqueline Beale-Delvecchio: "When my husband and I got married in 1995, hyphenated names were popular in our group of social justice–focused friends. I am the oldest of three girls and I did not want the family name to be lost. My husband loved his Italian heritage name as well. So we both gained a name and became the Beale-DelVecchios. Later we realized what the names literally mean—beale = handsome, good-looking, and del vecchio = of the ancient or old ones. So we are good-looking old people! I should also add that it was a one-day trip between the DMV, Social Security, and passport office in downtown Chicago for the both of us to change our names legally. Slightly harder for my husband because 'they' were not expecting that, but fairly effortless. We gave our kids our hyphenated name. We always teased that they would know the alphabet early on by trying to spell their name. They love their last name and plan to keep it—unless their partners have an even cooler name!"

Ángela Betancourt-Ciprian: "I've been married for four years and still have not legally changed my last name. I plan to eventually hyphenate it with my husband's last name but not sure when. Maybe when we have kids. I've kept my last name mainly because I am in the process of completing a doctoral degree and heard one of my mentors say once, 'I earned the degree, not my husband,' and this rang true with me."

Lori Ann: "I never feel bad about anyone's opinions. That's on them. I just follow my backbone. I have been married three times, and in each case, I changed my name legally as it's just easier for paperwork. But I always kept my name professionally, adding his to the end. We're joined. I'm not single. That's what I'm signaling. Signed, a card-carrying second-wave feminist."

Donna Martino: "I kept my name in both of my marriages. At the heart of it, the feminist in me never believed I should have to give up my identity to be someone's wife. I suppose if I hadn't liked my name—or didn't feel such a deep, positive connection to it—I might have considered changing it. But that was never the case."

## Exercise

I asked women how they would feel if their fiancé initiated a conversation about married name choices by saying:

"We need to discuss what name would be the best fit for our marriage name and family. I'm open to one of us taking the other's name, each keeping our own name, or any of the other options, including coming up with a new name for our new life together."

One woman told me: "If my husband said that, I would have been thrilled. It would show commitment and caring. It would show me, as the partner, that he understands this is a giant choice to make. It is a lifetime of change. I would feel very loved by someone asking that rather than making the decision all by myself. I also think if my husband and I had a real discussion, and maybe I got to hear how he really feels and that he hears me, it would have been more of an exciting moment of GETTING to take his name, rather than the heavy feeling I got because I felt like I had to. I feel like our culture just expects you to."

How about you? How would you feel if he initiated that conversation with you? Excited? Odd? Would you fall in love with him even more? Would you feel uncomfortable? Something else?

# *chapter six*

# SELF Reimagined

Imagine when the time comes to consider your married name choices, you understand the significance of your own name, you feel empowered to make the choice that aligns with your values, and you know the legacy you want to create and feel free to choose what's right for you.

How would that feel? Pretty powerful, right?

It's interesting that in the many conversations I've had with same-sex couples, either they start with the premise that they'll each keep their own surname or they make the "married name" discussion part of their wedding checklist, just like choosing the date and venue. They're modeling how it's possible to have these conversations, because they're not bound by typical gender norms.

When LGBTQIA+ couples discuss what last name to use once they're married, they approach the subject from a level playing field, knowing each person's name, and personhood, is equal to the other's. They talk about the significance of the name they were given at birth and whether it holds importance to them. They may also think about their future and how they would incorporate what's important to each of them in the last name they'd give to children.

Sara and Gwendlyn wanted to start their marriage with the same last name, and they wanted to have a family with one last name. They decided to take Sara's last name because they were very close to Sara's family and her German ancestry meant a lot to her. Gwendlyn's surname didn't have as much meaning to her because it was her mother's ex-husband's name. Not only did she not know the man or any of his family but also she didn't know where the name originated.

Hans told me that before he and his husband got married, they both assumed they'd each keep their own names. But Hans's name was very ethnic and hard to pronounce, so he asked his partner whether he could take his name.

"I asked him if he would mind if I changed my name to his once we got married," Hans said. "Since it wasn't my name, I wasn't just going to say I was changing my name to his unless he was okay with it. He was thrilled we'd be sharing a name together. We both feel more unified with the same last name."

Once gender is taken out of the "married name" equation, you're able to look at the topic in a whole new light.

## What's the big deal?

Some people ask me, What's the big deal? Who cares whether we continue to follow the same old tradition? Women have been taking men's names for generations. Why not just keep doing the same thing?

As Melinda Gates so eloquently says in her book *The Moment of Lift: How Empowering Women Changes the World*: "I think male dominance is harmful to society because any dominance is harmful: It means society is governed by a false hierarchy where power and opportunity are awarded according to gender, age, wealth, and privilege—not according to skill, effort, talent, or accomplishments. When a culture of dominance is broken, it activates power in all of us. So, the goal for me is not the rise of women and the fall of man. It is the rise of both women and men from a struggle for dominance to a state of partnership."

When women and men perceive a man's name—his identity, his ancestry, his history—as more important than a woman's name, we are really saying that men are more important than women.

According to Jennifer Worley, a licensed marriage and family therapist, when a woman in an opposite-sex marriage adopts her husband's last name, it can perpetuate a traditional, patriarchal view where the man's identity is seen as more significant. Worley feels this practice can have subtle but profound psychological impacts on women.

"Assigning greater importance to a man's name and identity can lead to feelings of diminished self-worth in women," Worley said. "When a woman feels her identity is less valued, it can manifest in several psychological issues or a sense of disempowerment. This is not just about a name; it's about the symbolic value attached to one's personal and family identity."

For women who retain their birth surnames, there can be a sense of maintaining individuality and a direct connection to their own family history, which can be empowering. But if the discussion doesn't continue to address what name to give children, the woman is still burdened with isolation and a diminished sense of power.

When we approach the subject of married names in the traditional sense, the man comes to the negotiating table with more power and clout. The idea that the man is head of the household, the protector, the enforcer is still so integrally woven into the fabric of our society that we unconsciously give men more power.

But if a woman and man come to the negotiating table on equal terms—I am as equally important as you—the power dynamic shifts. A woman can, and should, feel and say that her name, identity, ancestry, and history are equally important to those attributes of the man she's marrying.

That shift in power may seem slight, but it's actually huge. When you feel the weight of the suppression from the outdated tradition of giving up your name lifted, it's very possible you'll feel the repression lifting in other scenarios too.

## 50/50 by 2050

Imagine the day when studies show a 50/50 split between women and men changing their names when they marry, instead of the current 80% of women and 5% of men.

This would include a man hyphenating his name with his wife's or like the PenaVegas, combining the two names into one. It would also include men taking their wives' last name or the couple creating a new family name.

## How to Get to a 50/50 Split

You don't have to wait until you're engaged to talk about married name choices, and it doesn't just have to be with your boyfriend. I challenge you to start having conversations about this topic with friends, siblings, cousins, parents, children, and even the person who gives you a pedicure or does your hair. Are they changing their name? Why or why not? Would they consider hyphenating? Why or why not? Have they imagined creating a new name? Why or why not?

The fun starts if you can get the person to dig deep—below the tradition. Channel your inner 3-year-old self and just keep asking "Why?"

These can be fun conversations because there is no right or wrong answer; it's simply about sparking curiosity and empowering equality.

One woman told me that after we talked about married names, she decided she wanted to keep her birth surname in addition to taking her husband's name, so she decided to hyphenate.

"How would you feel if he also added your name to his, so you both hyphenate?" I asked her.

"I never thought about that option," she said. "I would really like that."

Of course, it's his choice whether he wants to change his name, but I encouraged her to share her feelings with her fiancé and present him with the opportunity to hyphenate his name with hers.

"He'll never change his name," she said, looking defeated.

"You have the right to ask," I encouraged her. "Continue the conversation. You could say something like, 'I understand you may not have considered adding my name with yours, but I would love it if you play around with the idea in your head. That way, when we have kids, we'll all have the same last name.'"

"He's already made it clear that our kids will have his name," she said sadly. "There's no reason for him to change his name."

"It sounds to me like you're giving your power away to him," I said. "Why is it his decision alone to choose your children's last name? Your name, your ancestry, and your identity are just as important as his. If he chooses not to hyphenate his name with yours, why can't the kids have the combined last name?"

## Starting the Conversation

Here are some tips you may want to consider when talking about this topic with your boyfriend or fiancé:

1. Feel empowered to ask for what you want and set boundaries.
2. Keep emotions out of the conversation; pretend you're discussing whether to have pink or mauve napkins at your reception.
3. Don't back down. Don't give in, but at the same time, be gentle, kind, and understanding. Think about it like deciding where to live. He wants to live in Wisconsin, and you want to live in Vermont. How do you decide?
4. Continue to search for solutions with mutual respect for each other's feelings.
5. Remember that your worth, identity, and ancestry matter.

According to Elvis Rosales, a licensed clinical social worker, the societal expectation for women to adopt their husband's last name is deeply ingrained in societal norms and can inadvertently lead to a power imbalance within the relationship.

"When a woman feels pressured to take her partner's last name, it might suggest a hierarchical structure that diminishes her identity," Rosales said. "Feeling as though one's identity is secondary or less important can contribute to reduced self-esteem and self-worth. It's crucial to approach this issue with sensitivity and understanding. Couples facing this dilemma should consider engaging in open and honest dialogue about their feelings regarding name changes. It's also beneficial for them to seek counseling or therapy, which can provide a safe space to explore these feelings and work toward a solution that respects both partners' identities and sense of self."

Cheryl Nieber, a licensed clinical social worker, said, "When women are faced with pushback from their mother-in-law, friends, or family members about whether or not to change her name, it can feel overwhelming because of interpersonal dynamics. My advice is to trust yourself. Seek support for communicating your feelings and stance. Be prepared to set boundaries and stick to them. Perhaps most importantly, remember that changing your name (or not) is a deeply personal decision. You get to be the expert here."

## Knowledge That May Help in Conversations

Of course, there are clinically correct ways to navigate difficult discussions with your partner, such as creating a respectful environment, using "I" statements, practicing active listening, and validating each other's feelings.

I'm not a therapist or trained professional in this area, so my tips may not be the most appropriate, but we're in the twenty-first century, and in my opinion, these questions/excuses/comments need to get with the times.

Here are talking points to some common conversation roadblocks.

### 1. *It's Tradition for a Woman to Take a Man's Name*

Traditions evolve as society broadens its social norms and customs. It was also tradition for the groom to stand on the left at the altar so he could draw his sword with his right hand to defend his bride. Times change. Traditions evolve.

### 2. *How Will Our Children Trace Their Ancestry?*

The same way women have been tracing their lineage for centuries: through the paper trail—birth, marriage, death certificates, etc. Besides, DNA tests are so readily accessible that tracing family history through surnames alone is a relic of the past.

### 3. *My Parents Will Be So Disappointed If I Change My Name*

I get it. Family pressure is real and can be a sensitive subject, but we're adults and we need to make decisions based on what's best for us, not our parents.

### 4. *Men Don't Change Their Names*

There are no laws requiring women to change their names, and there has never been a law requiring men to keep their last names when they get married.

### 5. *My Family and Friends Will Think I'm a Wimp*

What they say is a reflection of them, not us. What's most important is that we do what's best for ourselves and our future family.

### 6. *How Will People Know What Name We Choose?*

Let's think of a fun way to break the news to everyone. We could have a name reveal at the bridal shower or rehearsal dinner, like people do to announce the gender of a baby. Maybe we'll have people guess, then reveal our choice in a slideshow, beautifully crafted cards, or a large personal check with our new name in the "Pay To" spot. Of course, we can post it on TikTok and Instagram, and we can include it on our wedding website. How about we make a sign broadcasting our new name at our ceremony and have the officiant announce it right before we kiss?

Most importantly, intentionally choose a name together that brings you pride, have fun, and celebrate your married name!

# *References*

"About *Ms.*" *Ms.* magazine. https://msmagazine.com/about/.

"Baby Name Spessard." Nancy's Baby Names, February 20, 2015. https://www.nancy.cc/2011/06/14/baby-name-spessard/.

"Disney Princesses." Disney Royalty Wikia (Fandom), accessed July 4, 2025. https://dis.fandom.com/wiki/Disney_Princesses.

"FDR Biography." Franklin D. Roosevelt Presidential Library and Museum. https://www.fdrlibrary.org/fdr-biography.

"The Legacy of Joy Morton." The Morton Arboretum blog, January 13, 2022. https://mortonarb.org/blog/legacy-of-joy-morton/. tiktok.com+10.

"List of Matrilineal or Matrilocal Societies." Wikipedia, the Free Encyclopedia. Last modified June 29, 2025. https://en.wikipedia.org/wiki/List_of_matrilineal_or_matrilocal_societies.

"Maiden and Married Names." Wikipedia, the Free Encyclopedia. Last modified July 2025. https://en.wikipedia.org/wiki/Maiden_and_married_names.

"Quotations from the Speeches and Other Works of Theodore Roosevelt." Theodore Roosevelt Association. https://www.theodoreroosevelt.org/content.aspx?page_id=22&club_id=991271&module_id=339333.

"Remember the Ladies." Women and the American Story, Navigating the New Government, New-York Historical Society's WAMS. https://wams.nyhistory.org/building-a-new-nation/navigating-the-new-government/remember-the-ladies/.

Baswan, Meera. "The True Story Behind Disney's Pocahontas." The Indigenous Foundation, July 23, 2023. https://www.theindigenousfoundation.org/articles/the-true-story-behind-disneys-pocahontas.

Cheptegei, Zulekha. "Why Do Women Still Change Their Names?" BBC Worklife, September 21, 2020. https://www.bbc.com/worklife/article/20200921-why-do-women-still-change-their-names.

Coyne, Sarah M., Ashley Fonger, and Cora Rasmussen. "Disney, Superheroes, and Stereotypes." Psychology Today, September 2, 2024. https://www.psychologytoday.com/us/blog/the-right-media-mindset/202403/disney-superheroes-and-stereotypes.

Disney Princess Facts (@DPrincess_Facts). "Jasmine got married in the film Aladdin and is considered a Disney Princess. However, she is not officially part of the 'official' Disney Princess lineup." X, April 18, 2023. https://x.com/DPrincess_Facts/status/1646724964597510145.

The Female Quotient, the Knot, and SmithGeiger Group. "The Maiden Name Debate: Research Report." [n.d.]. PDF, accessed July 4, 2025. https://info.thefemalequotient.com/hubfs/The_Maiden_Name_Debate_Research_Report.pdf.

Film Ratings (Motion Picture Association). "MPAA Rating Rules." Revised 2023. PDF, accessed July 5, 2025. https://www.filmratings.com/content/downloads/rating_rules.pdf.

Fisher, David. "It's Time to Break the Chains of Being a Spinster." *Chicago Tribune*, December 4, 1994. https://www.chicagotribune.com/1994/12/04/its-time-to-break-chains-of-spinster/.

Gates, Melinda. *The Moment of Lift: How Empowering Women Changes the World*. New York: Flatiron, 2019.

Gough, Aidan R. "Community Property and Family Law: The Family Law Act of 1969." *Cal Law: Trends and Developments*, vol. 1970, no. 1 (January 1970). https://digitalcommons.law.ggu.edu/cgi/viewcontent.cgi?article=1057&context=callaw.

Harvard T. H. Chan School of Public Health. "Types of Bias, Ways to Manage Bias." June 2022. PDF, accessed July 5, 2025. https://content.sph.harvard.edu/wwwhsph/sites/2597/2022/06/Types-of-Bias-Ways-to-Manage-Bias_HANDOUT-1.pdf.

Haskell, Rob. "Jennifer Lopez on How She Found Happily Ever after for *Vogue*'s December Cover." *Vogue*, November 8, 2022. https://www.vogue.com/article/jennifer-lopez-december-cover-2022-interview.

Heching, Dan. "Kelly Clarkson Explains Why She Changed Her Name to Kelly Brianne." *People*, March 22, 2022. https://people.com/music/kelly-clarkson-name-change-late-kelly-brianne/.

Jacobs, Alexandra. "Chasing the Fairy-Tale Wedding." *The New York Times*, November 23, 2014. https://www.nytimes.com/2014/11/23/fashion/weddings/chasing-the-fairy-tale-wedding.html.

Lanks, Belinda. "Gender Stereotypes Begin at Age 10." Johns Hopkins Hub, September 7, 2018. https://hub.jhu.edu/2018/09/07/gender-stereotypes-child-development/.

Lin, Luona. "About 8 in 10 Women in Opposite-Sex Marriages Say They Took Their Husband's Last Name." Pew Research Center, September 7, 2023. https://www.pewresearch.org/short-reads/2023/09/07/about-eight-in-ten-women-in-opposite-sex-marriages-say-they-took-their-husbands-last-name/.

Maddox, Bentley. "Why Alexa Pena Vega and Husband Carlos Pena Vega Made Last Name." E! Online, December 12, 2024. https://www.eonline.com/news/1411046/why-alexa-penavega-husband-carlos-penavega-made-last-name.

Mahaney, Patrick. "In Alabama State, When a Woman Gets Married, Does She Have to Take Her Husband's Last Name?" Avvo, August 28, 2012. https://www.avvo.com/legal-answers/in-alabama-state-when-a-woman-gets-married-does-sh-890929.html.

Mann, Leslie. "What's in a Name? A Lot for Those Who Change Theirs." *Hartford Courant*, June 7, 2019. https://www.courant.com/2017/08/08/whats-in-a-name-a-lot-for-those-who-change-theirs/.

Michals, Debra, ed. "Lucy Stone." National Women's History Museum. 2017. https://www.womenshistory.org/education-resources/biographies/lucy-stone. mawomenshistory.org+13.

Morgan, Marcia K. *Should I Change My Name? The Impact of Your Last Name on Identity, Marriage, and Happiness*. Bend, OR: Migima, 2021.

Nelson, Camilla. "Friday Essay: Matrilineal Societies Exist around the World—It's Time to Look Beyond the Patriarchy." The Conversation, March 23, 2023. https://theconversation.com/friday-essay-matrilineal-societies-exist-around-the-world-its-time-to-look-beyond-the-patriarchy-200825.

Randle, Keirrah. "Man Legally Changes Last Name to Honor Stepfather, Surprises Him in a Video That's Gone Viral (Exclusive)." *People*, January 23, 2025. https://www.youtube.com/shorts/1IV1zvUPBow, https://www.tiktok.com/@keauramanifests888/video/7458488699647528222.

Risman, Barbara. "The Wedding Industrial Complex." HuffPost, August 29, 2012. https://www.huffpost.com/entry/the-wedding-industrial-complex_b_1636120?utm_hp_ref=email_share.

Rosenbloom, Stephanie. "A Patriarchal Tradition That Just Won't Budge." *The Atlantic*, October 27, 2021. https://www.theatlantic.com/family/archive/2021/10/patrilineal-surnames/620507/.

Shafer, E. F. "Hillary Rodham Versus Hillary Clinton: Consequences of Surname Choice in Marriage." *Gender Issues* 34 (2017): 316–332. https://doi.org/10.1007/s12147-016-9182-5.

Simon, Rachel. "Husbands Take Wives' Last Names." *The New York Times*, February 11, 2023. https://www.nytimes.com/2023/02/11/style/husbands-take-wives-last-names.html.

Slaughter, George. "Bush, George Herbert Walker." Handbook of Texas Online. Texas State Historical Association. https://www.tshaonline.org/handbook/entries/bush-george-herbert-walker.

*State v. Taylor*, 415 So. 2d 1043 (Sup. Ct. Ala. Apr. 9, 1982), rehearing denied June 11, 1982. https://law.justia.com/cases/alabama/supreme-court/1982/415-so-2d-1043-1.html.

Vena, Jocelyn. "Lisa Vanderpump Explains Why She Kept Her Maiden Name When She Married Ken Todd." *The Daily Dish* (BravoTV), January 28, 2019. https://www.bravotv.com/the-daily-dish/why-lisa-vanderpump-kept-maiden-name-not-ken-todd-after-marriage.

Vivinetto, Gina. "Miley Cyrus Shares Statement about Her Parents amid Family Feud Rumors." *Today*, June 12, 2024. https://www.yahoo.com/entertainment/miley-cyrus-explains-her-parents-060733385.html.

Willis, Jackie. "Zoe Saldana Defends Her Husband Taking Her Last Name: 'I Feel Proud.'" E! Online, June 9, 2015. https://www.eonline.com/news/664715/zoe-saldana-defends-marco-perego-s-decision-to-take-her-surname-hopes-to-redefine-masculinity.

Wolfe Bell, Erin. "Who Was Frida Kahlo, and What Was Her Connection to the Natural World?" Cultivate, Naples Botanical Garden, Spring 2023. https://www.naplesgarden.org/frida-kahlo-connection-to-natural-world/.

Wright, Paul J., Robert S. Tokunaga, and Betsy Woodworth. "Pornography Use, Sensation Seeking, and the Importance of Meta-Analytic Replication." *Sexuality and Culture* 29, no. 2 (December 14, 2024): 1007–1011. https://doi.org/10.1007/s12119-024-10299-9.

# Acknowledgments

It's been my dream to publish this book for many years. But over those years, I put it aside, convincing myself I needed to take another class first, or the timing wasn't right, or I heard a negative statement from someone and felt it was a silly idea. However, there were many people who encouraged and supported me to follow my dream and get my idea in print. I want to give a heartfelt thank-you to all those who cheered me on and invigorated me to keep going. There are so many to thank, but I want to give a special shout-out to the following.

I have to start with my first writing mentor, Cathy Stabelin, who suggested I tell my stories in the college magazine and newspaper. My confidence skyrocketed, and my passion to write was allowed to surface after pushing it down to have a steady, secure career in accounting. I learned so much from your brutally honest feedback and grew exponentially during those years.

In a close second, I want to thank my wonderful husband, Dennis. Not only were you open-minded and patient when I introduced the idea of our married name options, but you instantly got behind me and never doubted I would get my book published. You are truly my biggest supporter and best friend.

To my Monday night writers' group. You welcomed me with open arms, encouraged my writing journey, and helped me dig deep to make my stories stronger. And especially to Amy Abbott, who meticulously read through my first draft and helped me overcome my adverb addiction.

To Summer Bailey for sharing your professional editing skills. You're very gifted. And thank you Karen McKinney, for introducing me to you.

To Malinda Johnson and KC Kang for showing up on Thursdays this past year to keep me accountable and help me get to the finish line. Even though we spent only a couple minutes together, our promise to each other stuck with me from week to week to week. And Malinda, thank you for your insightful, detailed critique of my first draft. You helped me so much.

To Carol Cox and Diane Diaz from Speaking Your Brand for your genuine belief in me and expertise with my signature talk. It became the structure for this book. To Tiffany Hawk for your excellent book coaching skills and courses. And to both of you, Carol and Tiffany, for introducing me to the International Institute of Women's Voices Foundation and the other cofounding members—Vanity, Amy, Marian, Neha, Lana, Corrin, Kaylin, Christy, and Leili.

To CJ Redwine for your boost of confidence after reading my book proposal and for introducing me to your editor. Also for introducing me to Mary Weber of Cherry Pie Author Services. Mary, I could not have launched this book without you.

To my mom for reading all my articles and stories and always telling me, "That's nice. I'm so proud of you." You're the first person I want to show my work to, and your devotion has given me strength.

To the rest of my family, especially Kalie, Kevin, Keith, Katherine, Marcie, and Savannah. Thank you for always giving my social media posts a "like," even if only out of obligation, and never saying no when I ask, yet again, for another favor to introduce me to friends getting married, explain millennial trends, or read another chapter for me.

A big heartfelt thank-you to my bestie since high school, Lynn Garwood. Even back then you told me you loved my writing, and I thought you were the best artist ever. I love that our souls chose to be kindred spirits in this lifetime to watch each other grow into our artistic selves.

To Nancy Merkling for making me laugh and feel comfortable during our photo shoot. You're a great photographer who's not afraid to look goofy to get a good shot. Thank you for following up on my book and becoming an instant friend.

Also to Lisa E (with the complicated last name). Thank you for gifting me a photo shoot. I love the ideas you came up with and how easy it was to work with you.

Thanks to everyone on the Jenkins Group team who helped me. Special thanks to Leah, my patient publishing manager; Yvonne, my talented designer; and Devon, my precise editor who made sure my dyslexia didn't show. Thank you for your guidance, expertise, and hand-holding.

A big thank you to the talented and professional Brooke Schamerhorn, Chelsea Morgan, and Amanda Parsons. I used your full names so hopefully others will look you up and hire you!

And to Jennifer and Lucas of Pathway Book Services. You knew I just wanted to write and was a newbie to your industry. Thank you for your time, energy, and patience. You really know your stuff and really had my back.

To all the people who shared their stories with me. I loved hearing how you chose your married name and appreciate your time and openness. Thank you for trusting me.

And to all the other writer friends and contributors I met along my journey. Some of you I had only a quick conversation, while others I've known for decades. You showed up in my life and provided exactly what I needed at the perfect time. Thank you for being you. You're perfect just the way you are.

# *About the Author*

Melania Joy Murphy has been a journalist for over 25 years and has a degree in applied behavioral science. She's been published in numerous national publications and enjoys blending storytelling with research to explore identity, relationships, and the traditions that shape our choices.

Her personal experience with her own name fuels her passion for this topic. At 21, she took her husband's last name without much thought. Two decades later—after building a career, raising three children, and marrying again—she made the conscious choice to keep the name she'd grown into. Through this journey, Melania gained a deep understanding of the subtle but powerful pressures women face to follow tradition, even when it doesn't quite feel right.

With her foundation in applied behavioral science—the study of how people interact—Melania brings a sharp awareness of how often women set aside their own wants and needs to keep others comfortable. She believes out-dated naming traditions can quietly hold women back from stepping fully into their identity and becoming the most authentic version of themselves.

Melania has shared her insights as a guest on podcasts and as a speaker at women's groups, sororities, and bachelorette weekends, helping women and couples navigate their name choices with clarity and confidence.

This book is her invitation to rethink old norms and embrace new possibilities—together.

Born and raised in western suburbs of Chicago in a blended family where different last names coexisted, Melania now lives in Bradenton, Florida. When she's not writing or speaking about her book, she, her husband, and their dogs travel the country in their motor home, visiting their six children. Whether paddling through Florida's mangroves or walking the shoreline with sand between her toes, she finds peace in the water—and a glass of chardonnay at sunset never hurts.

To learn more, sign up for Melania's newsletter and download free resources, visit MelaniaJoy.com.

Author Photo Credit: Photography by Lisa E